THE TREASURE CHEST OF
THE EARLY CHRISTIANS

To my Mother

THE TREASURE CHEST OF THE EARLY CHRISTIANS

Faith, Care and Community from the Apostolic Age to Constantine the Great

DAVID BATSON

GRACEWING PUBLISHING
LEOMINSTER, HEREFORDSHIRE

WILLIAM B. EERDMANS PUBLISHING COMPANY
GRAND RAPIDS, MICHIGAN

First published in 2001
jointly

in England by   and in the United States of America by

Gracewing   Wm. B. Eerdmans Publishing Company
2 Southern Avenue   255 Jefferson Avenue S.E.
Leominster   Grand Rapids, Michigan 49503
Herefordshire HR6 0QF   www.eerdmans.com

All rights reserved. No part of this publication may be reproduced, stored in a retrieval system, or transmitted in any form, or by any means, electronic, mechanical, photocopying, recording or otherwise, without the written permission of the publisher.

© David Batson 2001

The right of David Batson to be identified as the author of this work has been asserted in accordance with the Copyright, Designs and Patents Act 1988.

GRACEWING ISBN 0 85244 522 9
EERDMANS ISBN   0-8028-3945-2

Typeset by Action Publishing Technology Ltd,
Gloucester GL1 5SR

Printed in England by MPG Books Ltd.,
Bodmin PL31 1EG

Contents

Preface		vii
Introduction		x
Chapter One	The Historical Background	1
Chapter Two	The Social Context of the Apostolic Age	14
Chapter Three	Jesus and the First Communities	25
Chapter Four	Charity Begins at Home	42
Chapter Five	Consolidation and Controversy	55
Chapter Six	Changing Fortunes	74
Chapter Seven	Constantine and the Christian Empire	100
Epilogue	The Roots of Community Care	114
Select Bibliography		120
Index		124

Preface

To study the life of the early Christian Church from its fragmented beginnings following the life and death of Jesus of Nazareth up to the established and developing organisation recognised by Constantine the Great in the fourth century is to embark upon a journey of discovery in pursuit, no less, of the religious and cultural roots of modern Europe and indeed the Christian world. The nature of the quest is likely to lead the unwary traveller into many false starts and along byways and devious routes which can confuse and frustrate those who expect a straight road, well signposted. The story of Christian origins is by no means clearly documented, scarcely at all in non-Christian sources and, when it is, rarely admits of simple interpretation. One thing is certain: none of the evidence should be taken at face value because, after two thousand years of Christian history, the inquirer will inevitably bring to the task the acquired 'baggage' of presuppositions and assumptions which must perforce be discarded before setting out. The traveller must proceed cautiously and as far as possible unencumbered. With that note of warning the journey can at least begin, safe in the knowledge that other more seasoned travellers are ahead to point out the pitfalls.

The history of the Mediterranean world in the Classical and Late Antique periods has attracted a great deal of popular interest in recent years, and the contemporaneous centuries of the early Christian era have also begun to be appreciated more widely for the rich mosaic they provide of personalities and events set against a background of imperial splendour. Early Christian history is no longer thought of as primarily the study of doctrinal formulation, of importance to the theologian or church historian but otherwise of scant interest to the general reader. Instead there is a growing fascination with a period that tells of the evolution of one of the world's great faiths, of the development of its corporate and social life and how its role as a carer of the needy has contributed in modern times to the concept of care in the community. This book is intended for the non-specialist, for the general reader who has an interest in how the Christian Church began and wishes to know a little more about how the earliest believers cared for the needs of the destitute and deprived in anxious and dangerous times, eventually providing a model of social care which was unique in Late Antiquity. It is a robust story of real people grappling with problems still faced by many in the world today. The dominant themes continue to resonate down the centuries: the relationship between Church and state, the divergencies between faith and practice, the conflict between traditionalism and modernity, the challenge of fundamentalism and the continuing reality of persecution. This, then, is a fascinating story as much as a study in social history. And like all good stories it inevitably leaves some questions unanswered. I hope the reader may feel interested by what is described all too briefly here to pursue those questions further.

The inspiration for the title of this book was taken from the translation of Tertullian's *Apology* in the Ante Nicene Fathers, vol. 3, p. 46, where the coffer in which the Christian communities kept the offerings of the faithful, *arca* in Latin, is rendered as 'treasure chest'. The translator has here captured the sense of Christians keeping safe the treasured alms, whether the widow's mite or the rich man's largesse, collected for the poor, themselves the real treasures of the Church. It recalls the delightful story of the deacon Lawrence, who, when asked by state officials to gather up and hand over the Church's valuables, assembled the poor and sick and said, 'here is the Church's treasure', and I am grateful to my editor for drawing my attention to this.

I owe an enormous debt of gratitude to the late Sir Steven Runciman, whom I got to know well only in the latter years of his long life. He read my manuscript, made many helpful suggestions and encouraged me in my endeavour. His library, to which he generously allowed me access, was itself a chest of great treasures. I am also indebted to Tom Longford, Jo Ashworth and the staff at Gracewing who have at all times proved courteous and constructive. To the following I also record my sincere thanks for their own individual and inestimable contributions: the late Father Hartley Brown, formerly Rector of Guarlford, Worcester; Noel Currer-Briggs; Barbara Docherty; Mary Donaldson; Miranda van Nieuwenhuizen; the late David Reynolds; David Rone Allen; also fellow members in the North American Patristics Society upon whose work I have been privileged to draw through the excellent Journal of Early Christian Studies and finally, several generations of social studies students who have always ensured that my feet were kept firmly on the ground.

Kindar House,
January 2001

Introduction

An important part of understanding the historical context of the caring work of the Early Church is an appreciation of the complex transitions it encountered across the broad spectrum of Classical and Late Antique society.[1] Its setting was the Graeco-Roman world which extended throughout our period from the Antonine Wall in north Britain to the edge of the Sahara Desert and from the Pillars of Hercules at the western gate of the Mediterranean Sea to the borders of the Persian Empire. It was a multi-cultural world, diverse and heterogeneous. The Celtic heritage on its western fringes derived from roots very different from the Hellenistic legacy of Alexander the Great or the oriental mystery cults that proliferated on its eastern frontiers. Yet over all, even at its remotest extremities, lay a veneer of Roman civilisation. Rome, the capturer of Greece, was at the centre of the known world and was itself enthralled by its captive; Greek culture permeated Roman life, Greek art and Greek thought dominated the Roman intellectual and artistic scenes. The phrase 'Graeco-Roman' came to personify Mediterranean life. It was a world that was no stranger to new and sometimes bizarre fashions in religion; it was at one and the same time hungry for change and eager to embrace fresh ideas, and yet was deeply conservative about what it held most dear, and deeply hostile towards those who sought to overturn the *status quo*. Christianity with its new social ethic and utopian promises challenged the stability of traditional pagan lifestyles and social structures, capitalising on the anxieties of the age. As a consequence it was made to suffer from outbursts of rage against it, but perversely seemed to draw strength from this. Within less than a generation it had spread from a provincial backwater to the heart of empire itself, it had produced a healthy crop of martyrs (always helpful to a cause that wants to make headway), it had raised a respectable debate in some of the larger cities of the empire about the burning issues of the day and it had begun to resonate, however faintly, across national and social boundaries.

What lay behind this apparent success story? A theme that recurs constantly throughout the first century is that of the transition of Christianity from its emergence in northern Palestine as a local movement revolving around the figure of a wise teacher who advocates an exemplary if eccentric lifestyle, to a renewal movement on the borderlines of Judaism speaking of future judgement and apocalyptic predictions, ultimately evolving into a cultic religion with a universal connotation. The factors that lie behind this process of development are both complex and controversial. Followers of the Jesus movement in the days of its infancy and early youth were acutely aware of the struggle to survive in an increasingly alien environment and therefore of the necessity to establish their credibility as socially and religiously conscious people with a message that needed to be heard. Judaistic lineage remained the movement's bedrock and inspiration until well into the second century and the Diaspora, the spasmodic dispersal of Jews throughout the Roman Empire, the means by which Christianity was assisted in establishing itself in key centres outside the Jewish homeland. A significant transition was already occurring. Divorced from its roots in the countryside of northern Palestine, questions were not long in coming about exactly how it all began and a mythology of origin was born which over the second half of the first century was to be committed to writing by the Synoptic evangelists, Matthew, Mark and Luke, followed soon after by the author of the Fourth Gospel and the first of the great Patristic writers. Key to this earliest of transitions was a small group of urban Jews who had encountered the teachings of Jesus, largely at second-hand, in and around the city of Jerusalem. Led by the Apostles Paul of Tarsus and Barnabas they took their own interpretation of the message away from the restricting confines of

Judaism to the Gentile world beyond and preached grander, one might almost say, universal themes of salvation and deliverance which frequently, but not always, found a ready and receptive audience.

Within Palestine itself increasing pressure was being applied by the puppet administration installed by Rome to suppress fledgling sects as potentially subversive movements, and it was all too easy for Jewish Christians to become tainted by association with those on the lunatic and nationalist fringes.

The part played by Jewish nationalism in the rise of Christianity is important to stress since it provides the historical context for political and social upheaval which rapidly spelt failure for the urbanisation of the movement on the soil of Palestine. Within the lifetime of the first generation of Christians, based in and around Jerusalem and still actively participating in Temple worship, the legions of Titus captured and partially devastated the Holy City, occasioning a mass exodus of Jews, including Jewish Christians. The result was to bring Jewish Christianity into closer contact with the Gentile (and pagan) world: a contact from which, paradoxically, all were ultimately to benefit. So, as the Jewish national revolt against Rome gathered momentum, the stage was set for the Christian message to begin its long journey towards official recognition; it was to take another two hundred and fifty years before it received the imperial imprimatur and much blood was to be spilled in the meantime.[2]

The expansion of Christianity over these early centuries coincided with the apotheosis of the Roman Empire, the consolidation of its power base and the emerging threat of barbarian incursion. The Principate of Augustus was a transitional link between the faded ideals of the Republic and the imperial aspirations of his successors.[3] If his own lifestyle was modest, as his title testifies, his ambitions for Rome and its people far exceeded it. The *Pax Romana* was more than just a jingoist slogan; it was believed to be and was seen to be a reality. Under Augustus the empire enjoyed an unprecedented period of peace; the price to be paid for it sometimes came high. The Jewish Zealots, for example, found the price of Roman peace too high to pay in the currency of nationalism. Their doomed struggle against the might of the Roman army allowed the early Jesus movement to take root well away from the main centres of conflict in the quieter conditions of rural Palestine and from thence to the cities of Asia Minor and beyond. It is easier to understand the attraction of Paul's message of the Reign of God heralding an eternity of peace and contentment against a background of social and political turmoil. An appeal of this nature was bound to raise expectations, but only for as long as the myth could be sustained and it was, to say the least, time-limited.

A sense of excitement and immediacy cannot be maintained indefinitely, and in the post-Apostolic age after the passing of Paul and Peter and their contemporaries the young Church found new emphases based on personal responsibility and ultimate salvation, on a new form of community and a heightened awareness of belonging to an élite, a world away from the traditional urban élites of Roman society. All this depended on following the stony and winding path of orthodoxy, the cornerstone of which was consensus, achieved largely through ecumenical councils, on the Nature and Person of Christ.[4] And this was a Christ of faith whose relationship to the Jesus of history paradoxically became somewhat obscured by the Fathers of the Church as they embarked on ever more precise and authoritative definitions. Thus the prolific output of their writings is sometimes, with justification, viewed as dry, technical and adversarial.

The intellectual battle between orthodoxy and heresy – begging the question as to what those terms precisely meant at any one time – once enjoined, was to preoccupy the finest minds of the Patristic Age, as indeed it has done ever since, resulting in the official support of a majority of the bishops for positions thus defined as 'orthodox': and marginalisation or, worse still, exclusion for those whose views were branded as heretical. But church leaders, whose overriding concern was the acceptance by the faithful of orthodox teaching, were themselves part of the social setting into which the Church had been born; their values were to a large extent its values, even if the faith they struggled to dogmatise and to which they were prepared to commit themselves body and soul set them apart from the norms of Graeco-Roman society. And the same held good for the young communities of Christians to which they ministered.

Not only did the first Christians share a faith based on belief in a Risen Saviour, a concept by no means strange to the ancient world, they also discharged a caring responsibility within their own localities that involved practicalities such as the provision of subsistence for the alleviation of poverty and distress, problems that were of first-hand experience for some of them. The social structure of the Early Church was broadly based, with the economically better-off tending to be located in urban centres and those in rural areas suffering the most disadvantage. What made the movement distinctive was the sense of common sharing, a practice that was enthusiastically adopted and became a *modus vivendi* in the early 'hothouse' atmosphere of rural Palestine, but which was never accepted in a wholehearted way in the urban centres of Asia Minor, as the apostle Paul was to discover. It is through his writings and those of the Christian leaders of the period that we glimpse the first Christian communities wrestling with the demands of practical Christianity and the resistance to changed lifestyles. In its earliest days in Asia Minor, Christianity was an urban and small-town religion that had moved away from its rural roots in every sense, and as its membership encompassed the complete spectrum of social classes it was inevitable that questions of poverty and wealth, for example, would be high on the agenda. Addressing these issues and their consequences for the everyday life of the young communities proved to be an ongoing task, and one which succeeding generations would require to consider anew.

The interaction between Christianity and its social setting in the period of AD 33–337 will form the substance of this book. Social life in the empire did not remain static; under the Julio-Claudian and Flavian dynasties the imperial system was new, and old Republican ideals died hard; the age of the Antonines, on the other hand, saw the consolidation of the role of the urban notables around the requirements of civic life where each town and city was virtually a little world of its own, illustrated by the story of the young boy who asked his father if every city had a sun like theirs! Under the Severans and the subsequent period of military anarchy the Graeco-Roman city experienced a slow and subtle change from traditional foundation to Christian community, so that by the time that Constantine came to set his imperial seal of approval upon the Church, he was to some extent recognising a *fait accompli*. Christians may have been a tiny minority, but they were here to stay.

NOTES

1. The use of the phrase 'Late Antique' requires some elucidation. Precisely what period of history are we covering? To begin with it is impossible to fix exact limits in a chronological sense either in respect of a *terminus a quo* or a *terminus ad quem*. The beginning of Late Antiquity overlaps with the classical period of Graeco-Roman civilisation under the early empire; indeed it might be argued that classical civilisation continued throughout the Late Antique era, since even up to the Arab invasions in the seventh century elements of 'classicism' were still recognisable in Mediterranean society. Scholars of Late Antiquity define the period differently. Peter Brown, for example, in *The World of Late Antiquity* begins his survey with the reign of Marcus Aurelius in the middle of the second century; whilst Averil Cameron in *The Later Roman Empire* suggests plausibly that it refers to the fourth to the seventh centuries. This book, in covering the period from the Crucifixion to the death of Constantine the Great, spans what we might reasonably describe as the Late Classical and early Late Antique periods. However, it is the continuity of the Roman world that should be stressed, rather than any convenient but artificial divisions of history. At least, as accurately as anything can, it can be claimed that the Arab invasions mark the closing of the Late Antique period.
2. See chapter 7 below.
3. Although the Principate of Augustus is regarded as the birth of the Roman Empire and subsequent bearers of the office styled themselves after him, he seems not to have thought of himself in 'imperial' terms; his title of Princeps is closer to First Citizen and the trappings of his office were correspondingly modest; his residence, for example, in the capital was an unpretentious urban villa.
4. The major Ecumenical Councils of the Christian Church did in fact achieve a remarkable degree of consensus on the principal

doctrines concerning the Nature and Person of Christ, considering the large number of variations current at any one time and the extreme passions these aroused even in the man in the street. Gregory of Nyssa, writing at the height of the Arian Controversy, said: 'If you ask about your change, the shopkeeper philosophises to you about the begotten and the unbegotten; if you enquire the price of a loaf, the reply is: "The Father is greater and the Son inferior," and if you say, "Is the bath ready?" the attendant affirms that the Son is of nothing.' Gregory did not just have his tongue in his cheek, religious debate took place at all levels of society. For an annotated index of the Church Councils see Ante Nicene Fathers, vol. 10, pp. 305–14.

Chapter One

The Historical Background

Hopes and aspirations have always dominated the lives of the people who inhabit the vital land bridge which links the northern and southern wings of the Fertile Crescent. But rarely have the hopes and aspirations been theirs alone. Throughout history their destiny has been entwined with the fortunes of their neighbours; in truth their very existence might be said to have depended to a greater or lesser extent on the rise and fall of those fortunes. Even today the natural corridor which lies between the Arabian desert to the east and the Mediterranean Sea to the west remains strategically and politically one of the most sensitive areas of the world.

The population of the Fertile Crescent is still as multifarious as ever in its history. Jews, Palestinians, Lebanese, Syrians, Arabs and Turks all compete for their share of the land and confront one another with rival and conflicting claims. At either end of the bridge lie powerful neighbours, Syria to the north, Iraq to the north-east and Egypt to the south, friends or enemies as fate decides. And it was ever so. As we consider the historical and social context into which Christianity was born we shall observe that the continual shifting of the balance of power in Middle Eastern affairs was the only constant factor. He who held the balance of power held the key to the region's future, and he who held the key stood at the crossroads between the oriental and occidental worlds and controlled the prosperity of millions.

First, then, let us look at the two most significant concentrations of power that dominated the Fertile Crescent prior to the arrival of the Romans. Until recent times Iraq was the 'land between the rivers', Mesopotamia, sustained by the

Tigris and Euphrates and called, without exaggeration, the cradle of civilisation. A glance at the map will show that Mesopotamia was itself a vast meeting ground for the trade routes from east to west, and its cities amongst the greatest trading places in the world. Inhabited in ancient times by a variety of nomadic elements which nevertheless form an ethnic continuum, Mesopotamia seems to have been settled since before the fifth millennium BC. This period, known as the Ubaid from the first site to have been discovered close to Ur of the Chaldees, was followed by the foundation of city-states in the fourth millennium in southern Mesopotamia. Subsequently we hear of the Sumerian people and of the Akkadians farther north and, from the third millennium onwards, of Babylonians, Assyrians, Amorites from the Syrian desert and, in the second millennium, of Aramaeans, a Semitic people who as a result of their extensive trading activities contributed the basic language spoken much later in Palestine.

To the south-west of the region lies the land of the Pharaohs. The two kingdoms of Upper and Lower Egypt are traditionally said to have been united by conquest under Menes, King of Upper Egypt, in the fourth millennium BC.

It was the sacred Nile, flowing north from the heart of Africa, that provided the life-blood and prosperity of the country and it was the king, an incarnate god, who controlled the annual flooding of its waters by the exercise of his priestly powers and thereby ensured the fertility of the land and the consequent welfare of its people.

For the sake of convenience we shall generally refer to the coastal strip that joins the two horns of the Fertile Crescent as Palestine, a name given in fact to only part of the territory as a result of settlement by the sea people or Pelestu (Philistines) in the thirteenth century BC. In reality, different areas were variously known as Canaan, Palestine, Judaea, Israel, Samaria, etc. according to early traditions about the peoples who settled there. Palestine thus linked the African and Asian continents and has been called 'a meeting place of many cultures',[1] an apt description, the significance of which will manifest itself constantly throughout the period we are studying. Egyptians, Babylonians, Assyrians, Persians,

The Historical Background 3

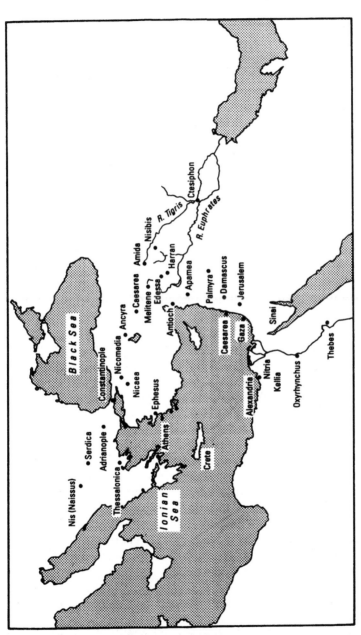

Map of the Eastern Mediterranean

Greeks, Romans and Franks, besides many other elements, all passed through the land and left their indelible marks upon it. Whilst the population over the centuries reflected this confusion of races it was dominated for a long time by a stock not of itself indigenous to the land. The Israelites were a semi-nomadic Semitic people whose founding father was the legendary patriarch Abraham whose family originated from Ur of the Chaldees in southern Mesopotamia and thence settled at Haran close to the northern Euphrates before finally moving down into Palestine.

Although a detailed account of the earliest history of the Palestinian peoples cannot detain us here it is important to recognise the extent to which geography influenced politics and social life and determined the processes by which the country became such a curious mixture of cultures and styles. Forged out of this was Judaism, the monotheistic religion of the Israelites, the natural parent of Christianity. A religion develops from the changing social consciousness of a group or tribe or even nation, any collection of individuals that might be bound together by a common purpose or driven by shared needs; it is susceptible to external forces that lie, invariably, outside its control. To give but one example: that Judaism managed to retain a degree of national exclusiveness, demonstrated by adherence to the Mosaic Law, in the face of the impact of Hellenism upon Rabbinical teaching, is a remarkable feature and of singular importance in the later history of the Jewish people.

Following the conquests of Alexander the Great in the fourth century BC and, after his premature death, the threefold division of his empire, the coastal strip of Palestine fell largely to his general Ptolemy. Ptolemy ruled from the newly-founded Egyptian city of Alexandria on the Nile Delta. However, the Seleucids of Syria with their capital at Antioch on the river Orontes, also claimed legal title to Palestine, which thus became a *casus belli* between 'the kings of the north and the kings of the south'.[2] For the Jews in Palestine a change of overlord was of lesser impact than the wider dissemination of Greek ideas that had first infiltrated a hundred years before Alexander and now greatly intensified. Indeed Hellenistic thought was rapidly penetrating the entire Middle Eastern world. In Palestine old cities were rebuilt with Greek names, and Greek was the language of educated men who met for discourse in Greek gymnasia and took their leisure in Greek hippodromes. Even the Hebrew Scriptures were translated into the Greek language in a version known as the Septuagint. Hellenistic philosophy and cultural life had become part of the fabric of everyday existence and the Jewish community was strongly divided between those who wished to adapt to new ideas and those who rejected all things Greek in pursuit of the moral purity of Judaism.

In 198 BC Antiochus III of Syria annexed Palestine, and his son Seleucus IV arranged for the most holy Temple of Jerusalem to be robbed to raise funds in order to meet the Roman demand for tribute. For his pains he was murdered and succeeded by his brother Antiochus IV Epiphanes (even more of a *bête noire* to conservative Jerusalem Jews) who made a determined effort to force the Greek way of life upon his new subjects, a misguided policy which culminated in an attempt to erect a statue of Zeus Olympios, bearing his own likeness, in the Temple. It was actions such as these, designed to Hellenise the Jewish people whether they liked it or not, that finally prompted the Jews to revolt under the leadership of the fiercely nationalistic Maccabean brothers Judas, Jonathan and Simon.

In their struggle with the Seleucid monarchy the Maccabees enlisted Roman help, a decision that was no doubt inevitable in the circumstances of the time but which in the long run was to cost the Jews dear. Certainly it was quickly to be regretted by the successors of the Maccabees, the members of the Hasmonean dynasty who, on assuming power, had revived the all-too-recently abandoned monarchy. For a time hopes ran high that the Jewish people were about to enter a more settled period of their history. But it was shaky from the start. The Hasmoneans, relying mainly on support from Judaea, the northern part of the Jewish state, quickly became unpopular. Although they eventually extended their rule over the whole area occupied by the old Israelite tribes, it was too narrowly based on ultra-conservative support for the Law and failed to attract the allegiance of the higher social classes and influential priestly families, many of whom had already embraced Hellenistic ideas. Moreover it alienated non-Jews, who resented having Judaism, and especially circumcision, imposed upon them.

Once again intervention from Rome was not long in coming. In 64 BC the Roman general, Pompey, successfully abolished the old Seleucid empire of Syria and annexed the area as a province of Rome; a deputation from Judaea visited him in Damascus, which included in its ranks representatives from Pharisaic circles, who entreated him to bring Hasmonean rule to an end. The request did not go unheeded. Pompey, deferring an intended campaign against the Nabateans, marched to Judaea by way of Pella and Skythopolis and thence moved on to Jerusalem. At first the inhabitants tried to refuse entry to his general, Gabinius, rather hastily changing their minds when the full might of the Roman forces appeared. The city gates were opened to admit Pompey who thereupon proceeded to behave in a brutal and insensitive manner, massacring those who continued to put up some resistance and then striding into the Temple and even invading the sanctity of the Holy of Holies.[3] Devout Jews felt outraged and the whole country utterly dispirited; they had paid a high price to get rid of the Hasmoneans. What they could not have possibly foreseen was that a turning-point had been reached in Jewish history, for it was to be two thousand years before a fully independent state of Israel was again to be established.

Most immediately, Pompey reduced the size of the Jewish kingdom and allowed the Greek population, dispersed by the ultra-orthodox Hasmoneans, to return to the cities of the coastal region and to the area known as the Decapolis. Inevitably there was a backlash from Jewish nationalists, who resented what they regarded as an unjust infringement of legitimate Hasmonean rights and property. Certainly the Roman action had caused social and economic distress amongst those Jews who had lost everything they possessed and in many instances were even deprived of their livelihood. Within ten years the Romans had appointed a procurator to govern the region.

From this point there begins an unhappy history of

Roman governorship in the new province of Judaea and its adjoining areas, a history of oppression and decline that was to culminate in the eventual fall and destruction of Jerusalem. The first of these rulers was Antipater, an Idumaean prince, whose people had been compelled to adopt the Jewish religion by the Hasmoneans and were thus not regarded by conservative Jews as entirely respectable. He had surfaced some years earlier when he supported the High Priest Hyrcanus and urged him to enlist help from the Nabataeans at Petra in maintaining his priestly office. Subsequently Hyrcanus was deposed and replaced, by Rome's greatest enemy, the Parthians, who invaded Syria and Palestine in 40 BC; but by this time Antipater's son Herod had already persuaded Rome to recognise him as 'king' of an extended Judaea which now included Galilee, Peraea and Samaria, although it was to be another six years before Herod gained control of Jerusalem itself (37 BC), then only to hold it with the aid of a Roman garrison.

Herod the Great, as history has come to know him, effectively secured his position by disposing of all other possible claimants to his throne. Despite highly ambitious building projects in Jerusalem and the founding of new cities to relieve overcrowding – in themselves no mean achievements – he incurred a lasting hatred from the people he tried to govern, a hatred which on his death turned to organised resistance. Guerilla tactics masterminded by charismatic leaders bore the stamp of either the freedom fighter or the terrorist depending on the point of view. The Roman point of view was unmistakably of the latter type. For the most part the Jews supported the rebellion, usually tacitly. Talk everywhere was of a long-awaited saviour, an anointed leader or Messiah. Rome's response was to put to death two thousand Jewish prisoners by crucifixion. This was 4 BC, the year of Herod's death and about the time of Jesus's birth.

The division of the client kingdom of Judaea between Herod's three surviving sons did nothing to lessen the hatred felt for the Herodian house on the part of the Jews; nor did it help reconcile factional interests in wider Palestinian society. Archaelaus, who had received Judaea and Samaria, was deposed in AD 6, whereupon direct rule of the territory from Rome was instituted in the person of a procurator; none of the holders of this office distinguished himself either by understanding the Jews or their religion (not in themselves the easiest of tasks), or by bringing some semblance of settled existence to the area.

After the disastrous attempt of the Emperor Gaius Caligula (AD 37–41) to abolish the practice of the Jewish religion at its most sacred centre, the Temple at Jerusalem, his successor, Claudius, sought to restore Jewish confidence in Roman rule by appointing Herod the Great's grandson, Agrippa, as king of his grandfather's former territories: in gratitude for Agrippa's earlier support of his accession, he increased the area of the client kingdom until it was almost coterminous with his grandfather's. Agrippa, who had been named after the famous Agrippa, friend of the Emperor Augustus, presented himself as a pious Jew, although in fact he had lived a life of not inconsiderable dissipation in Rome. In the event his reign was short – three years in all – and insignificant; he had behaved in an ostentatious manner and his professed religious belief was politically motivated rather than based on personal conviction; he died suddenly shortly after being acclaimed publicly as an incarnate god, heaven no doubt wishing to welcome him into the pantheon as soon as possible. His seventeen-year-old son was not allowed to succeed his father, and again the province of Judaea returned to Roman procuratorship; Agrippa's reign had been the merest of brief interruptions.

Sacred and secular powers of deeply opposing ideologies are able to coexist within a single state, if not always contentedly, at least with some accommodation that makes life tolerable for everyone; history records many such examples. The Jewish state under Roman rule is not one of them. Increasingly during the second half of the first century tensions grew into open conflict. In AD 50 Agrippa's son of the same name had received in compensation for Judaea his late uncle's kingdom of Chalcis in the Bekaa, together with the oversight of the Temple in Jerusalem. Moreover he could appoint the High Priest, a power that was controversial and much resented in some quarters. For the stricter and most conservative elements in the religious hierarchy a member of the Herodian family involving himself in Temple affairs was hard to swallow, although the young Agrippa made a show of upholding and promoting their interests.

Meanwhile Judaea, under a succession of unsympathetic procurators, began to decline steadily, discontent amongst the people leading to acts of rebellion, foretastes of the armed struggle to come. Israel's final and inglorious end was firmly in sight. After the dismissal of the third procurator, Cumanus, his successor, Antonius Felix, was hated as an adulterous despot, and anti-Roman feeling was further fuelled. Festus who followed him seems to have been the best of a bad lot, albeit for such a short period of time that nothing lasting was able to be achieved; his successor, the corrupt and rapacious Gessius Florus (AD 64–66), by his behaviour hastened the ultimate outbreak of hostilities.

It was Florus who, in AD 66, permitted the Roman military to raid part of the city with great brutality, after the Jewish community had derided him for removing money from the Temple treasury. The whole incident escalated and the people, urged on by the High Priest's son, Eleazar, came into open conflict with Rome. Agrippa's attempt to restore order by bringing in 3,000 troops was a complete failure and the rebels successfully seized the Roman fortress of Antonia in the heart of Jerusalem.

Our primary source for this period is the Jewish Roman historian Josephus, himself actively involved in the rebellion as commander of the region of Galilee until his capture by the Romans at the siege of Jotapata in AD 67.[4] During his captivity he was kept in close confinement by the Roman commander Vespasian, whom he greatly impressed; upon his release in AD 69 he remained with the Roman forces, being treated with much favour by them. Inevitably this gave rise to justifiable suspicion on the part of his own people and the levelling against him of accusations of treachery. Although on this evidence it is hard to escape the conclusion that Josephus was a turncoat, in his work on the Jewish War, *Bellum Judaicum*, he goes to some pains to demonstrate that it was Roman misrule that gave rise to the conflict as much as any long-standing disagreement about religious principles.

The future Emperor Vespasian had been put in charge of the suppression of the rebellion by Nero;[5] together with his son Titus they assembled a large combined force at Ptolemais, and soon the whole of Galilee fell into their hands.[6] Even at such a critical time when national unity was most needed the Jews in Jerusalem were racked by internal disputes, thereby encouraging the Romans to make the city the focus of the military operation. But for a time events back in Rome took a hand in delaying the final onslaught. On 15 January AD 69 the Emperor Galba, who had succeeded Nero in the previous year, was murdered and the empire embarked on what must have seemed the longest year of its short history.[7] No fewer than four incumbents occupied the imperial throne and it was Vespasian himself, who was proclaimed Augustus *in absentia*, who ended this fateful year with the hegemony of the Roman world. Such a change in circumstances required his presence in the capital in order to consolidate his position with the Roman people, and by the summer of AD 70 he was back home leaving the conduct of the Palestinian campaign to Titus.[8] The attack on Jerusalem was inaugurated in the spring of that year. Initially resistance was feeble and uncoordinated, with the city's ability to organise an effective defence greatly weakened by disagreements; indeed Josephus, in his partisan manner, says: 'old men and women, overwhelmed by the miseries within, prayed for the Romans to come, and looked forward to the war without, which would free them from the miseries within.'[9] But Josephus was not present to observe for himself, and his account of the horrors of executions and the bodies of the unburied dead is almost certainly exaggerated. Nevertheless, it is probably true that the imminence of Titus's final onslaught brought the inhabitants belatedly to their senses and forced them to put party differences to one side in a last-ditch attempt to defend themselves and their sanctuary. However, the time for concerted effort was past; when the end finally came and Titus took the city he is said to have exclaimed at the immensity of the defences, especially the towers, with the words: 'it is God who brought the Jews down from these strongholds,' a fitting but sad epitaph.[10]

With the fall of the three remaining fortresses of

Herodeion, Machaerus and finally in AD 73 Masada, whose inhabitants committed suicide, the long rebellion against Rome ended.[11] Accounts of the total devastation and depopulation of Jerusalem are again exaggerated, though it remains true that, excepting part of the walls and the towers of Herod's palace, much of the city was destroyed and the power of the religious leadership broken. The religious community continued as best it could amongst the ruins of the old city and the Temple, being joined eventually no doubt by new elements from outside, including Jewish Christians. Since the Sadducean priesthood had been bound up with Temple worship which was now scarcely possible, it fell to the Pharisees to reassemble the scattered remnants of the faith around the strict observance of the Law. A new supreme council based at Jamnia, the successor of the old Sanhedrin which had been largely dominated by Sadducees, was formed of seventy-two elders whose task it was to interpret and apply the Mosaic Law through teaching. Thus out of the necessity of the times was born the Rabbinical tradition of distinguished scholars and teachers.

The social and economic effects of these long years of rebellion and upheaval were deeply damaging and long-lasting for the people of Palestine, as the history of the Early Church bears witness. And with the fall of Jerusalem in AD 70 their problems were even yet not over. Josephus's *History of the Jewish War* ends with the events at Masada; of Jewish affairs over the next fifty years or so we know comparatively little; apart from occasional references in Rabbinical and Christian literature to political events we have to rely on writers like Cassius Dio (*c.* 163–235) to piece together the death throes of rebellion that lingered on for another half century, for even the tragedy of communal suicide at Masada did not quite extinguish the spirit of nationalism.[12]

During the reign of Trajan (98–117) Jewish insurrections broke out in various parts of the Middle East where communities had settled as a result of the Diaspora, and were suppressed with considerable brutality; but it was under Hadrian (117–138) that the last great uprising occurred in Palestine itself. Cassius Dio and the church historian Eusebius are not unanimous as to the precise reasons for it,[13] though it is likely that it was bound up with an imperial prohibition of castration by the Emperor Domitian which was renewed by Hadrian and confusingly included circumcision. The sources differ as to whether the prohibition gave rise to the revolt or was a punishment for it. If it were the latter then the real reasons for the rebellion remain unclear, apart from the possibility that it arose because of the establishment of the Roman city of Aelia Capitolina with its shrine to Jupiter on the site of old Jerusalem and the Temple. Hadrian is known to have established many new cities during his journeys around the empire, and on his oriental tour between 130 and 131 may well have decided to rebuild on the ruins of the Holy City. However, the rebel forces under Simon Bar-Kochba had some early successes, establishing themselves for a time in Jerusalem itself and even minting coins to celebrate the liberation of Israel. But early hopes of a Jewish restoration were quickly dashed by the vastly superior might of the Roman army. Simon died in the struggle and by 135 the old city and the surrounding land had been further devastated with great loss of life. So many of the population were sold into slavery that the market, usually a bottomless pit, was flooded and prices were at an all-time low. Hadrian's dream of a new Roman city raised to his honour was magnificently realised. Jews were forbidden to enter Aelia Capitolina on pain of death; the heart of the Jewish homeland and religion had become pagan; the province of Judaea once again became 'Palestine', in a most poignant sense, the land of the Philistines. So it was to remain throughout much of the period covered by this study and, as so often in its past, it was condemned to being a prey to the varying fortunes of the region.

NOTES

1. L. H. Grollenberg, *Shorter Atlas of the Bible*, p. 15.
2. *Ibid.*, p. 129.
3. In order to appease outraged Jewish feelings Pompey subsequently ordered the Temple servants to cleanse it.
4. Josephus, *Bellum Judaicum*, III. 204 seq.
5. *Ibid.*, III. 9 seq.

6. *Ibid.*, III. 110 seq.
7. The long year AD 69 began with the reign of Galba ҄ with Otho, Vitellius and finally Vespasian who was procla͆ Alexandria on 1 July in opposition to Vitellius. 'Statue ... illu͆ Galbae et Othonis et Vitellii longum et unum annum.' Tacitus, *Dialogus de Oratoribus*.
8. Jos. *Bell. Jud.* IV. 654 seq.
9. *Ibid.*, 10 seq.
10. *Ibid.*, VI. 423 seq.
11. *Ibid.*, VII. 176 seq.
12. Cassius Dio (*c.* 163–235), *The Roman History*, covers the period from the arrival of Aeneas in Italy to the age of the Severans, during which Dio served a second term as consul in 229 with the emperor Alexander Severus as his colleague. He died in Bithynia where he had spent the last few years of his life.
13. Eusebius Pamphilii, Bishop of Caesarea (d. 339). One of the most important figures of the late third/early fourth centuries and the major Christian source for the period. A fierce protagonist for Christianity, Eusebius has to be treated with some caution because of his tendency to overstate his case and exaggerate the facts. His numerous writings include the *Ecclesiastical History*, the *Life of Constantine* (*De vita Constantini*), in *Praise of Constantine* (*De laudibus Constantini*) and the *Martyrs of Palestine*.

Chapter Two

The Social Context of the Apostolic Age

The extension and consolidation of Roman rule throughout the lands of the Mediterranean seaboard is the dominant theme of the last fifty years of the pre-Christian era and of the first century AD. Imperial authority was upheld by the army and not infrequently destroyed by it. The army could make and break emperors, and increasingly did so during the period we are considering; it was therefore the major institution in Roman life to which all others were, in one way or another, secondary and subservient. In the provinces of the empire it was the legions which effectively policed political and social life and preserved the often precarious balance between national and local interests. Whenever those interests conflicted, as they very often did in the East, imperial authority was imposed with rigour and with little regard for its impact upon the inhabitants of the region. Its impact upon the society of Palestine and her near neighbours provides both the context and the conditions for the birth of Christianity – a phenomenon which is unlikely to have evolved the way it did had prevailing political circumstances been significantly different.

Roman provincial administration produced a variety of reactions on the part of its subject peoples, ranging from deep-seated and burning resentment to apathy and even a measure of desultory acceptance. Jewish reactions were mainly of the first type. As long as the purity of Judaism was upheld by adherence to the precepts of the Law and was centred on Temple worship in Jerusalem, then the fabric of Jewish society remained intact and the cohesiveness of national life unimpaired. The Jewish state had never cherished territorial ambitions beyond holding on to what it already had, namely the Promised Land of Israel. It was Israel's fate never to be left alone nor to enjoy anything approaching a lasting peace.

Conquest not only imposed an imperial system of taxation which became increasingly burdensome but also, by turning the land of Israel into a Roman province, inflicted upon it an authoritarian administrative machine that all too often was insensitive to Jewish religious susceptibilities. This was not in fact uniformly the case throughout the empire;[1] religious freedoms were usually respected by the Romans except in cases where they posed a direct threat to the stability of the empire; there are also many known instances of the Jews of the Diaspora receiving significant concessions from the authorities regarding the practice of their religion, including being permitted to build synagogues. But in their own homeland the Jews felt violated and despised.

We have seen already how, in the wake of the conquests of Alexander, Hellenistic ideas and culture were gradually assimilated by many Jews, except for a hard core of nationalists; Roman rule, by contrast, was, from the start, seen as being totally alien. Rome was nothing less than an unwelcome occupying power and the benefits of law, administration and citizenship were to most Jews no more than fringe benefits, as the Apostle Paul amongst others was amply to testify.[2] Nevertheless Roman rule was a reality and Roman Law prevailed.

The application of the law lay in the hands of the provincial governor as presiding magistrate; he determined in the name of the emperor and the Roman senate whether an act was to be judged legal or illegal and therefore whether a charge could stand or not. Some provincial governors were confused, in the absence of clear guidelines, about what constituted a criminal act. The classic and much-quoted example from the early Christian period is that of Pliny the Younger, Governor of Bithynia, who wrote to Trajan seeking clarification as to whether Christians could be charged for simply admitting to be Christians or whether resultant behaviour, such as refusing to offer incense to a statue of the emperor, should be held to be criminal. The imperial advice when it came did little to dispel the confusion.³

At any rate the governor with the local garrison under his command acting as a police force dealt mainly with more serious cases, such as major public disorder, and left lesser legal issues to the jurisdiction of local officials according to the long-established laws and customs of the area – as, for example, happened with the Sanhedrin and the High Priest in the province of Judaea whose authority was supported by their own Temple police. It suited the empire very well to divide up jurisdiction in this manner, since it allowed Rome to maintain control in matters vital to state security whilst preserving a semblance of local autonomy in respect of less threatening offences.

In some instances, however, the role of native law enforcers is less easily defined. Cases in point from the New Testament would be the execution of Jesus and the subsequent death of the first martyr, Stephen, recounted in the Acts of the Apostles. In the case of Jesus, while the death sentence was demanded by the Jewish religious authorities it was administered by the Romans; there has been much debate over the historical accuracy of the gospel accounts relating to this and it may well be that they have been 'treated' to fit in with the overall purposes of the gospel writers and editors. Pontius Pilate, the Roman provincial governor, seems ill at ease about the legal process and reluctant to pass the death sentence, implying that the public disorder caused by the activities of the Jesus movement was of a minor nature. His attitude provokes the Jewish leaders to outrage and Pilate, to appease them and no doubt to avoid the risk of greater disturbance, after some hesitation accedes to their demands. The incident provides valuable insight into the strength and importance of the movement at its moment of inception and confirms the view that it was intended to be a peaceful renewal movement rather than a force for political change.

Somewhat different circumstances surround the death of Stephen. Taking the evidence at face value, the native powers, in this instance the Sanhedrin, seem to have assumed the necessary authority to impose capital punishment despite the fact that Rome had clearly transferred this responsibility to itself throughout the rest of the empire. One view is that this may have been a case of spontaneous corporal punishment that went too far and resulted in death, and we are reminded of what happened to the apostle James the Less at the hands of the chief priests in AD 62. It seems highly unlikely that Rome, usually unwilling to encourage independent action, would have effectively put extra powers of criminal jurisdiction into the unpredictable hands of local leaders.

Stephen's death, recounted in chapter 7 of Acts,[4] could well be a case of persecution that got out of control in the heat of the moment. Pre-conquest, death by stoning was prescribed for certain offences, for example adultery; Stephen's declamation and accusation of intransigence against his fellow countrymen so infuriates them that they evict him from the city in a hail of stones which inflict fatal injury. In the aftermath of the incident a more general persecution against Christians in Jerusalem starts up and many are forced to flee the city to take refuge in outlying rural areas. If Stephen's death was essentially accidental then the ensuing action is perhaps more easily explained as in part a perverse justification for what had earlier taken place. Assuming this to be the case, it would suggest that the Jesus movement was regarded as socially uncomfortable and therefore unpopular because it was not seen to be backing the religious establishment.

At all levels of law enforcement under the empire a wide range of punishments was available: financial penalties; beatings; imprisonment; and death by sword, by crucifixion or in the gladiatorial arena were variously used under some kind of unofficial tariff, although in practice the actual disposal often depended on the whims of the magistrate. Under Mosaic Law for Jews both corporal and capital punishment was prescribed for certain offences and death was by stoning – although, as noted above, it is uncertain whether the Romans permitted this to continue in Judaea.

Social life in Palestine in the lifetime of Jesus and in the subsequent period, referred to as the Apostolic Age, was thus conditioned by the Roman legal system as well as by certain existing laws and customs of the old Jewish state which were allowed to continue. But ecological factors played an even more significant role in determining the daily existence of the population. To begin with, a number of natural disasters occurred in or around Jerusalem over a one-hundred-year period up to AD 70. An earthquake in 31 BC which virtually destroyed the livestock of the area was followed two years later by a terrible epidemic. Then in the thirteenth year of Herod the Great's reign (25–24 BC) there was a prolonged drought followed by a further epidemic of plague and the failure of the cereal harvest; not only did the diet of the population suffer as an inevitable consequence but there was even a shortage of clothing because of the unavailability of wool. Famine again struck the region during the reign of Claudius (AD 41–54), and over the four years preceding the destruction of Jerusalem by Titus in AD 70 there were at least two further devastating droughts.

The frequent occurrence of such wide-scale natural disasters had the effect of weakening the economic infrastructure of Palestine and bringing about social circumstances which polarised factional interests only too prepared to exploit an already disadvantaged and discontented underclass. The time and conditions were ripe for rebellion; all that was required was the arrival on the scene of a few popular leaders able to mobilise the hotheads amongst their followers, usually political activists waiting only for the right time and opportunity to organise and move. It would have been comparatively easy for the aims of the Jesus movement to have been deliberately misunderstood by those unsympathetic to it and for it to be tarnished with the reputation of being subversive.

By and large the underclass was to be found in the rural communities which tended to suffer most from the deprivations that followed in the wake of natural disasters; resources to mitigate the worst effects were few and diminishing across the once-Fertile Crescent and tended to be concentrated on the main centres of population, such as Jerusalem. Even Jerusalem was exceptionally hard hit by the Claudian famine, enduring a degree of severe economic distress from which it was never to recover; on this occasion, we are told, the Christian community was helped out by its better-off brethren in Antioch. When we consider that these events occurred within a decade of the crucifixion of Jesus and that therefore the Christian movement must have been very much in its infancy, certainly organisationally, it is worthy of remark that it had already developed a strong enough sense of solidarity and cooperation to be in a position to respond to a humanitarian need of this kind from a group of fellow-Christians who were clearly in trouble. The foundations of care in the Christian community were already being well and truly laid.

Of course, Jerusalem had always been problematic in times of difficulty by reason of the fact that it possessed a woefully inadequate water supply, coupled with a lack of accessibility to necessary raw materials; at times of extreme hardship individual rulers, of necessity, stepped forward and played a key part in the relief. Josephus tells how both Herod the Great and Agrippa I adopted the role of benefactors and, particularly in the latter's case, made considerable personal sacrifices for the good of the country.[5] Less admired, for the manner in which it was carried out, was the action of the procurator Pontius Pilate who ordered the building of an aqueduct for the city with funds controversially acquired from the Temple treasury; in the event it proved an insufficient means of bringing water within the walls of the capital in the absence of its own natural springs. No further attempt to improve the situation seems to have been made until the mid-second century when one additional water conduit was built to serve the needs of the new Roman city of Aelia Capitolina, when it arose on the ruins of old Jerusalem.

Although the establishment of the *Pax Romana* brought a new kind of political unity to the Mediterranean world there was no correspondingly new direction for economic affairs. Augustus introduced little by way of significant change but allowed the old *laissez-faire* system of the Republic to continue throughout the empire. There was no need for state controls, monopolies or interventionist policies because Rome – and, indeed, the whole of Italy – had become progressively more prosperous, particularly during the Augustan era and consequently dominated the rest of the imperial world. Nevertheless, a simple economic principle applied throughout the whole of Late Antique society: the economic and social basis of Graeco-Roman civilisation rested on the *quid pro quo* principle: favours were done, favours in return were expected and the debt of allegiance was established.

Reciprocity was accepted as part of friendship between equals, but was a requirement between social superiors and their social inferiors. Patronage, the traditional system of protection and support, lay at the very heart of classical life; community prosperity depended on the personal investment of wealthy patrons who in their turn were under a moral obligation to contribute to public expenses. And contribute they did, to public works and public pleasures, sometimes in gestures of great magnificence and generosity that considerably enhanced the prestige of the community and raised its standing in the eyes of outsiders. This type of patronage has been called *euergetism*, private liberality for public benefit. It should be distinguished from the private patronage of individuals whereby social inferiors or *clientela* attached themselves to a wealthy patron in order to gain some form of social benefit or advantage on a purely personal basis. The *clientela* were not necessarily poor: the patron himself in fact might well be the *cliens* of a social superior, and the procedure could continue right up the line to the emperor himself at the pinnacle of the social pyramid.[6]

Most commonly, support was given by the patron to the individual *cliens* in the form of food or money; there was no question of any stigma attaching itself to this type of donation, nor was repayment required in kind, but the expectation was that it would be returned in intangibles like loyalty, respect or political allegiance, and less intangibly in actual votes. Clearly, what the Graeco-Roman world regarded as 'patronage' would for us, in twenty-first-century terms, be tainted with the smell of corruption. The patronage system in effect allied the dependent *cliens* to his patron, thus making him a part of his dependent circle. Donations in kind tended to be made to those who would be able to make the most return; if the genuinely needy, in a very basic received anything by these means it was entirely incidental and was not regarded as being the primary purpose of the gift. 'Charity', as we understand the term today, was virtually unknown in the Graeco-Roman world, which was why the Christian community was able to establish caring strategies of a practical nature to address the needs of those at the very bottom of the social and economic pile who were in no position to repay patronage either tangibly or intangibly and hence were excluded from this preferential system.

Orthodox Jewish society, on the other hand, as represented by the synagogue and its surrounding community, adhered to a somewhat different moral principle. Charity, in the sense of almsgiving, had always been an important feature of Judaism, although a general precept in the first century was that a limit should be set to charitable giving amounting to one-fifth of the giver's means. It is not entirely clear from the gospel records whether the teaching of Jesus upheld this strict principle, or whether his injunction to 'sell everything you have and give to the poor' represents a call to asceticism on the part of the Jesus movement by pushing the boundaries of giving to their ultimate extent. It has to be remembered that the members of the movement were itinerant missionaries (or, 'wandering charismatics') rather than community organisers,[7] and as such had given up possessions and a settled way of life for that of the travelling evangelist dependent on the charity of others for daily maintenance.

Amongst the Jews, therefore, private charitable giving extended across the social spectrum. At one end of the scale the ruling families contributed considerable personal wealth, whilst at the opposite end the widow's mite was not to be despised; we are told that in Jerusalem worshippers of all kinds on their way to the Temple would give alms to a beggar or food to a poor lunatic;[8] indeed, this kind of charitable giving was considered especially praiseworthy if performed by pilgrims. Much of the private charitable assistance thus described was donated for the express relief of misery and want in times of national disaster, but, quite apart from this, charity also extended into the public domain. Both the Torah and Rabbinical legislation prescribed conditions for relieving the lot of the poor which obtained whether times were hard or not. Provision was made for the remission of debts in the Sabbatical (seventh) year and in the third and sixth years of seven a tithe of harvest produce was ordered, as well as other entitlements during harvest-gathering time, such as gleanings, fallen grapes, thinnings, etc. The Talmud, moreover, in listing social regulations that may go back to the time of Joshua, laid down that a man could graze his cattle in woods, gather wood in private fields and fish in the Sea of Gennesaret when need arose.

Provincial life in the empire was centred on the urban communities and services were geared to the needs of urban populations. In Jerusalem, for example, most of the arrangements for relief were based on the Temple, which took good care to look after its own but at the same time made certain concessions to the poor, as in the more modest offerings permitted in cases of hardship. Special consideration was also given to widows and orphans – a cause, as we shall see, particularly dear to the hearts of early Christian communities and illustrated by the fact that, under the regulations of the Jerusalem Talmud, a widow could remain undisturbed in her marriage home if her husband had so willed it (by implication, the opposite case at one time must have held true, rendering widows not so protected extremely vulnerable). In the course of time this right was extended throughout the country whether provided for under the terms of a will or not, thus removing a major disadvantage for women.

Both the public and private aspects of charitable giving amongst the Jews may be said to derive from a well-established ethical system that we can see being worked out in the Old Testament writings. It was a direct result of life experiences recounted in the pages of Jewish history, presented as a gradual revelation to God's chosen people of His immutable will. Hence, carrying out God's commands and doing a good deed for its own sake, regardless of any profit it might or might not bring, were the foundation stones of Jewish values, in marked contrast, as we can now see, to the

Graeco-Roman system of patronage with its crude *quid pro quo* principle.

In the Hellenistic-Jewish society into which Christianity was born there was a constant tension between the traditional observance of the Mosaic Law interpreted by Rabbinic teaching and based on synagogue worship, and the standards, values and attitudes of the Graeco-Roman world. To complicate our understanding of these matters even further, over the centuries since the conquests of Alexander a good deal of syncretism had occurred between the many cultural and religious movements that abounded in the Middle East. We have, however, to be careful when describing Palestine as a social and cultural melting-pot, not to imply too great a sense of sophistication of thinking, almost of a maturity belonging to a nation 'come of age'. This would be a wholly misleading impression to convey of the nature of society in first-century Palestine. The country was overwhelmingly comprised of small agrarian communities, traditionally following the social and economic patterns of life established over many generations, and largely untouched by the changing styles of the urban centres of population. Within the larger cities such as Jerusalem or Caesarea or the towns of the Decapolis new ideas indeed circulated and permeated public life and influenced views about the nature of the world and of religion, but these barely penetrated the villages of rural Palestine.

It is in this latter milieu that the Jesus movement began and where during the lifetime of its founder it enjoyed its greatest success. Only when the movement attempted to extend its mission into Jerusalem were its aims misunderstood, and it came into violent conflict with the religious establishment. If, therefore, as we have already claimed, the Jesus movement, as distinct from the mission of Jesus himself, can truly be said to be a renewal movement internal to Judaism, then its rise was part of a radical response of ordinary people resulting from the failure of Jewish-Palestinian society to integrate with the empire of Rome. Such movements were not uncommon in the first century and covered the entire spectrum of religious and political opinion; the Jesus movement represented the more

24 The Treasure Chest of the Early Christians

quietistic and socially-aware wing of such popular views, whose moral precepts were internalised and directed towards renewed and strengthened relationships within Jewish society.

NOTES

1. See Michael Grant, *The World of Rome*, p. 44 seq.
2. Paul used his own status as a Roman citizen to good effect on more than one occasion. See Acts of the Apostles 16.35 seq., 22. 25–29.
3. Pliny the Younger (*c*. 62–113). His letter to the Emperor Trajan was written *c*. 112 (Pliny, *Epp*. X, *ad Traj*. 96). Trajan's reply ran as follows: 'They [Christians] are not to be sought out; if they are informed against, and the charge is proved, they are to be punished, with this reservation, that if anyone denies he is a Christian and actually proves it, that is by worshipping our gods, he shall be pardoned, however suspect he may have been with respect to the past.'
4. See Acts of the Apostles 7.8–60.
5. For Herod the Great's benefactions see Jos. *Bell. Jud.* I.407 seq. and for his grandson Agrippa I see II. 223 seq.
6. For a fuller discussion of this subject see *Patronage in Ancient Society*, ed. by Andrew Wallace-Hadrill and *Bread and Circuses* by Paul Veyne, trans. by Brian Pearce.
7. See p. 37 below.
8. Acts of the Apostles 3. 2 seq.

Chapter Three

Jesus and the First Communities

Trying to obtain a coherent picture of the patterns of everyday life in the Church is not an easy task because the earliest communities of believers were not ecclesiastical organisations as we might understand that phrase in a modern context; formal structures developed relatively slowly, more so than the New Testament seems at times to imply. Of course, some degree of rudimentary order was required from the start to address those basic issues faced by all organisations at their genesis: questions of leadership; seniority; conduct in assembly; and, as we have seen, contributions to the community chest for the relief of the poor. To begin with, Christianity was a personal matter that touched individuals in its appeal to the heart and mind, extending thereafter to those closest to the individual – families, groups of friends or neighbours, whether of high standing in the community and socially secure or lower down the social and economic ladder, 'ordinary' men and women with children to raise and homes to run. In precarious times not a few at the bottom of the heap would find themselves dispossessed and without means of support; some, in all likelihood, would have disabilities and hence be unemployed and unemployable. Orphans and widows are often referred to as especially disadvantaged groups, being deprived of the family breadwinner, alongside those who were too sick or too old to work, and as socially powerless they would have been intensely aware of what it was like to live on the fringes of a society where the bare necessities of survival were not easily accessible. Thus it was the most deprived sections of the

Christian community, the recipients of charitable giving, those without power or influence, who all too frequently became the inevitable pawns in the games of religious controversy.

It is hard for us to imagine that the more esoteric levels of theological debate could possibly have impinged on the lives of the Christian 'poor', but we find that all too often they were caught up in the consequences of changing fashions and ideas, occasionally acrimoniously and even disastrously so; religious matters were openly discussed at all levels of society, and religious life, which was a fundamental part of everyday life, was no more free of the vicissitudes of fortune than any other aspect of human experience. Real power, however, in both Church and state, was concentrated in the hands of a few brokers who controlled the means upon which the poor depended for subsistence. Leading families and individuals for whom the ownership and management of land and property was the benchmark of their social status, held the key to the survival and happiness of the underclasses. The Roman jurist Ulpian, who lived during the reign of Alexander Severus and acted as one of the emperor's chief advisers, tells that sometimes the wealthy kept their warehouses fully stocked with grain precisely so that they could drive up the price in times of famine and hardship, an obvious example of social and economic control deployed for their own benefit and to the ultimate detriment of the poorest in the community. This type of malpractice was still very much in evidence in the mid-fourth century, when Basil of Caesarea, the Cappadocian bishop, inveighed against it in more than one Sunday sermon (see below p. 115). Christian attitudes towards the poor were clearly very different, though not all Christian communities were necessarily free of the charge of exploiting a situation to their own advantage.

Charitable acts, however altruistic, were sometimes an opportunity for the powerful to assert their status and thus open the door to the abuse of position. St Paul, for example, reprimands one prominent Christian community where the least deserving take advantage of the commemoration of the Lord's Supper to indulge themselves whilst others go hungry. He was clearly scandalised by what had been reported to him about those in the community who were turning the occasion into a party, whilst those in real need were being excluded. From the tone of the Apostle's rebuke we may speculate as to whether this was a case of the better-off in the community using their influence to obtain some return on previous investment![1]

The principle of charitable giving as practised by the Early Church must have been viewed by Graeco-Roman society at large with scepticism if not disbelief. Despite imperfections in the system it attempted to address real need and to ignore social divisions; nothing comparable existed elsewhere nor was its ethical basis part of the Graeco-Roman way of life. However, setting standards that could be applied across numerous scattered Christian enclaves over a vast geographical area, often with very different cultural traditions, posed problems for church leaders. It seems as though some Christian communities adopted a method of charitable giving that was closer to the patronage system, well established in Roman society, than it was to the prevailing practice of possessing all things in common that characterised the Palestinian Christians, nevertheless claiming for it an essentially Christian ethos. On the internal evidence of the Epistle to the Romans, this appears to be the situation Paul encountered in the Gentile Christian communities which owed their foundation to him or to one of his associates. He tells us, for example, that prior to his planned journey to Rome he would first be depositing in Jerusalem a generous financial contribution for the poor collected by Christian communities in Macedonia and Achaia (Rom. 15. 23–26). When he later writes to the Corinthians he urges a similar generosity upon them, citing the example of these communities who he says, 'gave not only as much as they could afford but far more and quite spontaneously.' These are not glimpses of communities in which there is common ownership of property and money, but ones where additional collections were made from the personal resources of individual members, who were apparently prepared to stretch themselves to the uttermost to come to the rescue of needy brethren in a desperate plight. So the Apostle affirms both the motive for the collection, as well as the manner of it, and he goes on to express the hope that the 'saints' (that is, the Christian community) in Jerusalem will accept it. No doubt the Jerusalem 'saints' did accept the gift in the spirit in which it was made, because at a time of real crisis when there was little or nothing to share out from the pool of their own resources, outside intervention must have come as a truly saving act. The Gentile Christians of Asia may have held that the moral basis of their charity was firmly rooted in the teaching of Jesus but actually it owed little to his concept of 'love-communism'[2] and far more to what has come to be called 'love-patriarchalism',[3] a notion that will be explored more deeply below. Herein lies a significant difference which we must appreciate when examining the patterns of social care in the Early Church, for we are faced with an apparent conflict between two underlying philosophies of community support, the one based on the time-honoured principle of patronage, the other on the concept of a new model society. The first depended on power, how it was exercised and by whom; the second required the repudiation of all power relationships: the nature of Late Antique society was such that there was bound to be a clash.

Even before the first generation of Christian leadership had passed away, the inevitable conflict had crystallised in a number of different ways, as can be seen from the respective stances of Gentile and Jewish Christians. As far as the latter were concerned the new movement which had sprung from the peripatetic teaching of Jesus would be most effective as a pressure group within Judaism, a positive force for change inside the old order. Its constituency would be Jerusalem and the rural milieu of Palestine where, particularly in the unsophisticated countryside, the practice of 'love-communism' might become a reality. Paul and his itinerant missionaries on the other hand preached a message which, unlike the Judaisers, had to gain acceptance in mainly urban Gentile settings albeit with a significant resident Jewish core. This core constituted the missionaries' first line of approach together with Gentile 'God-fearers', converts or quasi-converts to Judaism, who had attached themselves to local synagogue congregations (see p. 38 below). The charitable structure that evolved, and which came to fruition under Constantine, was closer to the concept of 'love-patriarchalism' and essentially Pauline in nature. However, at the outset the caring work undertaken by the Church in protecting its own vulnerable members like widows and orphans, seems to have contained both the best and worst features of the two models, but somehow it worked and was an influential factor in the appeal and consequent expansion of Christianity.

The message of the Jesus movement, or the *kerygma* as it is known (from the Greek *kerugma*, meaning a 'proclamation' or 'public notice'), contained in essence the germ of the new model society, a society moreover that was synonymous with the Kingdom or Reign of God. With this proclamation a new age was to be ushered in, a new deal was to be offered to humanity. The *kerygma* was to have clear implications for the lives of those prepared to listen: the hallmark of the new society was the affirmation of the belief that Jesus of Nazareth was the Christ, risen from the dead and exalted to the right hand of God; its ultimate vindication lay in the expectation that the present order of things would soon be brought to a glorious conclusion. All human effort, therefore, needed to be directed towards preparation for this cosmic event. This is the unequivocal message of the New Testament, namely that the proclaimed Christ of faith was to be found in the person of the historical Jesus: he was the necessary catalyst for the arrival of the new age, the Divine instrument of God's saving work. This had come a long way from the simple preaching of Jesus's Galilean mission.

Over the passage of time this eschatalogical thinking, which had had its roots in Jewish Messianic expectations about the end of the world, underwent considerable revision as hopes were not immediately realised, with the result that the Church was to concentrate its mind on a new set of priorities concerned with orthodox belief and organisational life in the social conditions of an increasingly divided and destabilising world. The extraordinary growth of the Church in the first and second centuries is consequently perhaps less of an historical phenomenon than is sometimes portrayed, given the prevailing background of religious, political, social and economic factors. Conditions, particularly in the eastern half of the empire, worked to the Church's advantage in many instances; for example, the Jewish Diaspora in AD 70 following the fall of Jerusalem was important to the rise of the new faith and to its dissemination, since up to that point many Jewish Christians were to be found amongst practising worshippers at the Temple; when this became no longer possible they gravitated to other urban centres outside Palestine. Again after the Bar-Kochba War (132–35) there was a further and even greater dispersal of Jews from Jerusalem and its environs which, as before, included Christians of Jewish birth, and whilst Galilee became the new stronghold of Palestinian Judaism, the Christian element infiltrated the cities of Asia Minor and Egypt.

The Acts of the Apostles provides us with a somewhat idealised account of early conversion statistics, but then it was intended to serve a clear apologetic purpose and needs to be read in that light; a more realistic appraisal of the increase in numbers suggests that initially Christianity's influence was at best patchy and seems to have been most evident in the cities of Asia Minor long accustomed to the rise of new religious cults. The Near East had always been a religious melting-pot, and this is where Christianity succeeded in making an impact, possibly because of its cross-cultural appeal and perhaps – is it too much to suppose? – because it provided an answer to the problems of the human condition that transcended social and cultural barriers.

In certain respects, of course, the new faith was a synthesis of the most powerful religious themes of the age – salvation, redemption, deliverance from one's enemies and even the promise of ultimate vindication in this world or the next. In our own sceptical times, the extent to which ancient society took these ideas on board and took them very seriously should not be underestimated. But there was even more to it than that. From the very start of the movement, as has been observed already, the scattered Christian groups, little more than isolated gatherings of believers in many instances, still maintaining the traditional practices of their Jewish faith through synagogue worship, demonstrated an acute social conscience, directly derived from the Mosaic Law but heightened by the moral teaching of Jesus with its strong emphasis on personal righteousness and the obligation to care for neighbours and strangers alike. Perhaps what should be emphasised therefore, is the continuity of social concern between the new communities and the charitable work of pious Jews, which provided the primitive Church with an effective model upon which to base its own system of poor relief (see below pp. 44–46). The Christian message was thus set within the historical context of Judaism, an integral part of which had always been the primacy of the family and the community; overarching these commanding themes was an unswerving monotheistic belief which may be said to have formed the foundation stone of the Jewish state.

However, in the earliest days of the Jesus movement, it was not the moral and social aspects of his message that presented a challenge to the Jewish establishment and threatened to disrupt the *status quo*; indeed, the claim that Jesus himself was a social revolutionary who tried to subvert traditional values is not borne out by the key elements in his teaching. The message as preached was unequivocal but hardly subversive: with the dawning of a new age things are bound to change; the old order is not being overturned, rather it is being transformed, and human relationships should henceforth be reflections of man's relationship with God. On the face of it this seems straightforward enough, scarcely the stuff of which revolutions are made, yet it disturbed the religious establishment and attracted the increasingly unwelcome attention of the secular authorities. As to why, we may only speculate. Part of the answer must lie in the deteriorating political situation in Palestine, linked to the fact that although the ministry of Jesus had mainly been concentrated in the villages and amongst the rural population it had begun to resonate with a wider circle of his contemporaries who, according to St John's Gospel, may have been influential in encouraging the movement to shift its focus to Jerusalem, where it was inevitably going to acquire a rather higher profile, albeit with tragic consequences (John 7.2–3).

There was another aspect of the Jesus movement which perhaps came closer to the charge of social disruption. The *kerygma* also sounded a warning that those who decided to follow the new way might well face some upheaval in their personal and family life: when a loved one chose to depart from the faith of his or her forebears it was likely to occasion fuss of a fairly considerable kind. In short, families might become divided and members set one against the other; not the sort of message to encourage domestic stability. Christianity's overtly divisive nature, however, owes just as much to the narrow conflicting interests of party groups as it does to anything contained in the preaching of Jesus. There were famous clashes between universalists like Peter and Paul and the Judaising party in Jerusalem, as the Book of Acts wryly tells us.[4] Bitter were the arguments that broke out all too frequently in Christian assemblies, disagreement centring around issues of faith, order and practice, as for example the admission and circumcision of Gentiles wishing to join the ranks of the faithful, in which the strict traditional view represented by the Judaisers was effectively superseded. Whilst battles royal such as these were destined to become an increasing feature of Church life, they seemed to have had little discernible effect on evangelistic success.

The Gentile cause had as its supreme champion Paul of Tarsus, whose great achievement was in pioneering the spread of the Christian Gospel to many of the major urban centres of Asia Minor and Greece, where its appeal increasingly caught the imagination of every social class. The scale of such heroic work itself raises the question of the nature of that appeal; here was something more than the advent of just another cult, especially one revolving around the figure of an obscure dead Jew said to have risen from the grave following a degrading execution. Did it offer more than vague promises for a better future? Actions appear to speak as loud as words in this pragmatic new movement, and its principle of common sharing, at least in theory, might open up the possibility of an innovative social system. But then again there were soon to be question marks against those who declined to pay the customary courtesies to the emperor: loyalty to the state was at stake here; a new cult was all very well, but not one that threatened the established institutions. These must have been amongst the many questions raised in people's minds by the new faith, questions that cut across all the contemporary issues and involved religious belief, economic pragmatism, social administration, juristic government and ethics.

Christianity's remarkable attractiveness began with a simple proposition. It offered an alternative way of coming to terms with a complex and frightening world, a way that was socially more equitable and morally more achievable than the existing conventions of Graeco-Roman society. Its credentials lay in being able to transform a very parochial Jewish movement into a universal creed that was not tied by narrow cultural apron strings to its Palestinian past. Israel as a nation-state had been in eclipse for several generations, and with the events of the late first and early second centuries its final demise was assured. And Judaism, all its long history of moral vigour apart, had, through the experience of the Diaspora, become even more narrowly legalistic as it, in turn, adopted a less aggressive proselytising style in its struggle to survive in an alien world.

In any event, Judaism as a community-based faith with a racial identity was bound to hold little attraction for non-Jews. Even militant Islam at a much later date was to prove incapable of matching in quite the same way Christianity's true sense of catholicism.

The genesis of Christianity occurred shortly after the Roman Empire had entered its most aggressively expansionist period. Rome was a militarist state and hence totally dependent upon the maintenance of a vast army. By the middle of the second century AD it had already become preoccupied with the defence of its own hard-pressed borders as the barbarian tribes of northern and eastern Europe began to nibble away at the edges. Successive emperors, therefore, were faced with the problem of continually raising levies of troops and trying to pay them, which not infrequently they failed to do. Paradoxically, one solution, increasingly adopted from the second century onwards, was to recruit mercenaries from amongst the barbarian tribes themselves in order to curb the incursions of other barbarians. But this served only to open the floodgates to barbarian settlement in the Roman west with long-term consequences that were, by the fifth century, to change irrevocably the political map of the empire. Meanwhile, rising prices and a collapsing silver currency compounded a deteriorating political situation, and although Diocletian, through his price-fixing measures, was to attempt the most radical monetary reform the empire had ever seen, its success was short-lived and was probably a case of 'too little, too late'.

The requisition of goods from local populations to satisfy a soldiery whose irregular wages bought less and less every day imposed a burden on society which resulted in large numbers of casualties, with corresponding degrees of vulnerability and disadvantage. Against the background of such conditions the new faith of those who called themselves Christians not only held out the promise of a better deal when the expected new age should come – and some people genuinely believed it was just around the corner – but offered immediately a degree of practical care in difficult times that other secular or religious systems were unable to match.

The earliest groups of Jesus's followers, both those of Jewish birth based in and around Jerusalem as well as Gentiles from farther afield, consequently embraced and passed on to their successors the ethical basis of his teaching enshrined in the memorable aphorism, 'Love God and love your neighbour as yourself'. In essence, one must accept that this was not a wholly different concept from that taught in good Roman households: to respect the gods and family and friends and be a good citizen in one's local community. At the heart of both there is a sound social ethic which keeps society together and guarantees stability. But for the Christian Church its application went much further. It resulted in the development of strategies for caring that were distinctive enough to endow the Church with the reputation for being a socially-conscious movement, a unique status in the Graeco-Roman world. Forms of charitable relief did, of course, exist in the Roman Empire. The patronage system, although designed on a *quid pro quo* basis and excluding the very poorest who had nothing to offer in return, did enable some who might have been temporarily embarrassed to retain their foothold on the social ladder, but that is as far as it went in helping the 'needy'. Apart from that, in the principal cities and towns both in Italy and the provinces, local craftsmen set up guilds to protect their own trade and to look after dependants in those families where the male wage-earner was no longer around, thus rendering them economically helpless. Otherwise there was little or no protection available for the unemployed, the disabled or, indeed, for displaced persons who inevitably constituted a significant part of such a vast and heterogeneous empire. Daily distributions of corn and other foodstuffs for poor relief were a common enough feature of Late Antique society but these were designed mainly to act as emergency provision in times of national famine and hardship; at all other times the population was expected to provide and fend for itself.

In the writings of the Fathers of the Early Church the picture we may hope to see of a practical caring organisation can often seem obscured by the attention apparently paid to questions of correct belief and individual salvation rather than what we might regard as the really urgent problems of the time. It is all too easy to read our own priorities back into history and assume that what is important to us in the early twenty-first century was important to our Christian forebears in the first or second centuries. Whilst expectations of the early return of the Saviour and the imminence of God's reign remained alive, longer-term issues, such as the attitude towards property and riches, were to some extent kept in the background, but all the evidence seems to suggest that they did not remain there for long. Caring for the Christian poor presented immediate logistical problems that required a unified community response and it has already been suggested above that two broad approaches were followed: one of sharing all things in common in the early intense 'hothouse' atmosphere of rural Palestine which was closest to the scenes of Jesus's life and ministry, the other approach of 'means-tested'[5] contributions to the community chest being more appropriate to the cosmopolitan conditions in the urban centres of Asia Minor and beyond. The author of Luke–Acts is at pains to illustrate the two situations: in the

Gospel Jesus's care for the 'delinquent' classes is a recurring theme, whilst the book of Acts shows real interest in how the problems of poverty and wealth impinge on the Church's social life.[6]

Outside the corpus of the New Testament one of the most important early documents is the *Didache* or Teaching of the Twelve Apostles, apparently a type of manual of church practice and moral instruction and valuable to us for the insights it affords into the everyday life of early Christian communities.[7] Otherwise documentary evidence for the social thought of the young Church is scanty, with the consequence that it is to secular sources one must turn to obtain a fuller picture, especially for the political background of the period, an understanding of which is an essential prerequisite to a mapping of social trends. As far as references to Christianity are concerned in the classical (pagan) authors, these are few in number and tend to be restricted to accounts of conflict between Christians and the imperial authorities.

'These are the men who have turned the world upside down', was said of the first Christian missionaries, and why persons of such diverse backgrounds from every stratum in society, men and women, (the latter were sometimes the means by which Christianity was able to infiltrate the upper social classes) were drawn into the movement and even became its leaders is a question that lies at the very heart of the Gospel's appeal. Christianity, with its foretaste of things to come, was a salvation religion – it promised deliverance from evil in an age when evil was perceived as tangible and real and was only too evident on every side. If salvation could be achieved by a profession of faith in God the Father and His Incarnate Son through the operation of the Spirit in the rite of baptism, and if the redeemed soul gave witness to this by the performance of good works, then there were many only too prepared to follow these parallel paths to eternal life and to go out and encourage others to do the same. The personal cost of commitment to the missionary life was considerable, involving loss of status and employment, in all likelihood loss of family and friends, the certainty of a precarious existence for those who chose the life of a wandering charismatic preacher or indeed took upon themselves (or were commissioned) to fulfil the role of a community organiser. In both instances there lurked the possibility of rejection or an even worse fate.

'Wandering charismatic' is a useful description for a particular type of missionary to be found mainly in the early days of the fledgling movement when it was still revivalist and Jewish in nature in the immediate post-Crucifixion period. It is a term that has come to be favoured by some theological writers in recent years to distinguish between the different types of missionary activity in the Early Church.[8] Wandering charismatics can be recognised in two ways: first, their itinerant evangelistic preaching marked them out from the run of Jewish society at that time and identified them with various groups which renounced many of society's norms in favour of alternative lifestyles; secondly, subsistence was provided for them on a day-to-day and village-by-village basis as a fair return for their inspired preaching to a susceptible and eager rural population.

By way of contrast, the 'community organiser', represented most vividly by figures like Paul and Barnabas, carried the mission beyond the confines of Palestine to the Hellenistic cities of the eastern empire and Asia Minor. In this kind of social setting the work ethic was strong, and equally strong was the condemnation of the so-called 'begging' of the wandering charismatics. Hence the community organiser whose work involved the establishment of Christian groups or house churches in these major urban centres was expected to earn his keep by following a normal trade or profession – Paul was known to practise his trade as a tentmaker. The exceptions to this were those who had been compelled to give up their normal occupations, such as farmers or fishermen, in order to become evangelists and who were therefore entitled to support from the communities they served. The point has been made that the mission to the Gentiles brought the community organisers into contact with people from entirely different traditions from their own Judaistic background, and that consequently a degree of independence in financial matters was advisable. Since it would take the Christian missionaries some time to become accepted, if at all, in an alien culture, they themselves were at pains to avoid the danger of their essential message becoming confused with questions of subsistence; there were already plenty of itinerant teachers and philosophers in circulation and in need of support – perhaps in some cases even on the make – to bring missionary activity into disrepute.

The technique of the early missionaries on arrival in a new location was to make contact with the resident Jewish community, through the synagogue if there was one, or if not via the Jewish quarter. This gave them an instant point of reference from which to reach out to the Gentile-Jewish converts and hence to the non-Jewish population, which initially meant groups of artisans and their families. Converts to Christianity therefore first heard the message by means of personal contact and a 'cell' was established. The way was thus open for the missionary to be introduced into widening circles in the life of the city which were likely to be Graeco-Roman and not exclusively confined to the lower social and economic classes. Since the usual meeting place was someone's house, the size of the group was determined by the size of the room available. This clearly also influenced the ethos of the group by facilitating a sense of sharing and commonality, as well as providing the setting for the development of the Church's liturgy, the shape and form of which owes much to this early type of social gathering.[9]

Here it is worthwhile commenting on the references above to Gentile-Jewish converts. In many of the cities of the empire to which Jews had consistently emigrated during the course of the first and second centuries AD there were to be found small but, for the Early Church, significant numbers of Gentiles who had attached themselves to local synagogues and had become known to orthodox Jews as 'God-fearers', attracted no doubt by the Jews' monotheistic faith, by their strict sense of morality and strong family life, and perhaps above all by the charitable work they undertook on behalf of their co-religionists. More of a problem to these Gentile converts were the Jewish rituals of abstinence from eating pork and the practice of circumcision, and even their refusal to sacrifice to the emperor, which could cause painful misunderstanding. It was, however, for these and other reasons that this group became the prime target of the missionaries for conversion to Christianity and from which therefore the very first converts were secured. As the Jews in the cities of the Diaspora clung to their traditional observances, the God-fearers proved only too ready and willing to take on board a new faith which retained some of the best features of Judaism without the disadvantages.

Religion and politics are frequently disapproved of as topics of dinner-table conversation, probably wisely, because they have always been inextricably linked and abidingly controversial. Things were scarcely any different for the early Christians. Jesus had been executed by the Roman governor acting under pressure from the Jewish religious authorities, yet it was Rome, not the Jews, that the Early Church held responsible. Over the years, as conversions to the Christian faith were drawn much more from the Gentile than the Jewish world, the Church's attitude was to change and the Jews came to be held to blame for the Crucifixion, a situation that was to continue until recent times. But to begin with it was the might of Rome that brought Jesus to the gallows and challenged the subsequent survival of Christianity. Conflict with the state seemed endemic in the new religion for the simple and good reason that it divided loyalties and therefore threatened national security. How else are we to explain, at least in part, the fact that the Jews for all their separateness were frequently accorded a degree of tolerance and freedom of worship in many of the cities of the empire that was all too often to be denied the Christian Church?

No universal religious movement, and that is what Christianity set out to be, could possibly achieve credibility without martyrs to the cause.[10] The Church did not have to wait long. Stephen the Proto-Martyr died as a result of stoning in around AD 35 and most of the major figures amongst the leadership were soon to suffer a similar fate;[11] there were many others of the rank and file of whom we know little or nothing who joined them on the road to martyrdom. Yet Rome was not necessarily intolerant of religion as such. In may respects its own state paganism had become something of a formality, albeit one that was taken seriously by the establishment if not always by the man in the street, and was closely bound up with oaths of loyalty to the emperor as head of state. Romans could never quite understand why Christians, unlike some other religious minorities, found this a problem. Sacrificing to the emperor was a courtesy, an act of politeness, an expression of respect, rendering unto Caesar the things that are Caesar's, not an issue to go to the Arena for. Yet for the Christians it proved an insuperable barrier. The essence of the difficulty was not the paying of respect – Christians had always been taught to do that – but the physical act of sacrificing to a statue and then being obliged to eat the sacrificial meat. By refusing to comply with this requirement the Church declared just where its allegiance lay, and from this point on it was to find itself on a collision course, the seriousness of which would mostly depend on the attitude of local magistrates and rulers and the overt behaviour of Christians themselves. Only when the emperor himself took up the cause against the Church, as happened under Nero and Domitian and again in the second and third centuries, did persecution become for a time a matter of state policy. What amazed the Roman authorities was that the Church turned it into a virtue and positively thrived on it. The dominant themes that influenced the growth and expansion of the Church over the first three centuries were to recur, albeit in different guises, until the dawning of the Middle Ages in western Europe, and in the east even beyond the darkest days of the seventh century when the Byzantine Empire confronted the Arab invader.

NOTES

1. I Corinthians 11. 17 seq.
2. See Martin Hengel, 'Property and Riches in the Early Church – Aspects of a Social History of Early Christianity, chapter 4 "The Love-Communism of the Primitive Community",' in *Earliest Christianity*.
3. This concept derives from Ernest Troeltsch, *The Social Teaching of the Christian Churches*, London, 1931, 2 vols., reprinted New York, 1960. See also, Gerd Theissen, *The Social Setting of Pauline Christianity*, chapter 2 – 'Social Stratification in the Corinthian Community: A Contribution to the Sociology of Early Hellenistic Christianity'.

4. See Acts of the Apostles, 10. 44–8 and 11. 1–18.
 5. The modern phrase I employ here requires a brief explanation. I wish to lend added strength to the notion that donors were expected to conform to an accepted tariff of what was an appropriate donation in accordance with their known resources. It had always been a basic tenet of charitable giving that the individual should contribute according to his or her means and quite often those who attempted to conceal the full extent of their holdings incurred a heavy rebuke. This applied equally in Jewish society as it came to do in Christianity, but right across the ancient world the concept of a tithe, namely the tenth part of a revenue, was widely held to be a general guiding principle. Of course, the Church tried to emphasise the value of voluntary giving as especially meritorious and Jesus himself on at least one occasion is said to have counselled a rich young man to sell up all his possessions and give them to the poor as a precursor to discipleship. But this was exceptional. Robert M. Grant, *Early Christianity and Society*, p. 134 seq.
 6. For a fuller discussion, see Henry Cadbury, *The Making of Luke-Acts*, SPCK, London, 1958.
 7. For easy reference see 'The Didache – Part I, The Two Ways' in *Early Christian Writings* trans. by Maxwell Staniforth (Penguin Classics).
 8. For a full discussion of the terms 'wandering charismatic' and 'community organiser' see Gerd Theissen, *The Social Setting of Pauline Christianity – Legitimation and Substance: An Essay on the Sociology of Early Christian Missionaries*. Although Theissen's theory has been reassessed by various scholars since it appeared in 1982, it remains influential. See also article by J. A. Draper in *Journal of Early Christian Studies*, vol. 6, number 4, 1998: 'Weber, Theissen and "Wandering Charismatics" in the Didache'.
 9. Gregory Dix, *The Shape of the Liturgy*, Dacre Press, Westminster, 1943.
10. For further reading on the persecution of Christians in our period, see Marta Sordi, *The Christians and the Roman Empire* and Giuseppi Ricciotti, *The Age of Martyrs*. Sordi's work is the more critically objective of the two; sadly, Abbot Ricciotti's suffers from, at times, an over-literal English translation.
11. See pp. 16–17 above.

Chapter Four

Charity Begins at Home

Given the diversity of cultures and social settings amongst which early Christianity was established, it is perhaps not surprising that in very few respects was the emerging Church an homogeneous unity from the outset. The outlines of a 'catholic' or universal Church begin to be discernible only by the end of the second century with the general desire, for reasons of credibility and survival, to move towards a consensus on doctrinal matters (never in fact achieved), on an established order of ministry and on the settlement of the canon of New Testament scriptures. Over the first one hundred years of the Church's existence the priorities were bound to be different, with the most important elements of the new faith focusing on the practical application of Jesus's message to daily life as a preparation for the eagerly-anticipated 'second coming'. Yet whatever sense of urgency lent itself to motivating the performance of good works as outward demonstrations of belief, ultimate salvation was held to rest on an individual's profession of faith in the Risen Christ. That was the bedrock upon which a Christian life was to be built and of which all else was but an inevitable consequence. In examining the actual strategies for caring that were adopted by the earliest communities of Christian believers we must not lose sight of the fact that for them faith in Jesus of Nazareth as the Christ and loyalty to his name were the prerequisites for the Christian life, the *sine qua non* for the justification of subsequent behaviour. What could not possibly have been foreseen was the fact that these strategies effectively became the foundations of the Church's longer-term role in society.

The preaching and mission of Jesus set the tone and pace

of the renewal movement; the style and scope were his alone and it is unlikely that he himself intended the universalising of his message outside Judaism, at least in the movement's immediate future. Although Judaism was the setting, 'I was sent only to the lost sheep of the House of Israel', for the times were urgent for the Jewish people and the days were evil, Jesus's broader vision was subsequently seen as embracing the whole brotherhood of mankind in which a renewed Israel would be the catalyst for the final establishment of the Kingdom of God.

If the Kingdom or Reign of God was thought to be imminent then, inevitably, attitudes towards riches and property would be conditioned accordingly.[1] God and Mammon made conflicting and mutually exclusive demands upon people, as the Beatitudes and many of the parables make clear. From the same mould are Jesus's strictures to those who seemed overly anxious about the satisfying of everyday needs which, he averred, could safely be left in the hands of God, as was borne out by his own peripatetic mode of life. Yet Jesus, as we have said, was no social revolutionary;[2] he took for granted the social divisions of the society in which he lived – which were exacerbated under the Romans and their Herodian client kings – especially the marked differences between the landowning classes and the small farmers or landless tenants. Wealth was not entirely to be despised but could be made to work for the good of society as a whole, and indeed his own mission was to a large extent supported by a number of well-to-do women who attached themselves to his circle, an unusual departure from the social mores of the time.[3]

Possessions therefore should be used to help those in greatest need in the community. This is the intention behind Jesus's injunction to the rich young man to sell off his property and thus freed from worldly encumbrances to join his band of itinerant followers.[4] After all, the inner circle had effectively adopted this precept, including breaking with their families to serve the cause of the Kingdom. This was a good deal more than mere social protest or dropping out of a society with whose values one felt out of sympathy. Nevertheless it was perceived as being socially disruptive, as Jesus's actions against the money changers in the Temple seem to bear witness, and, as we have already remarked, became in Roman eyes a legitimate justification for the subsequent execution of Jesus as a rebel, despite the fact that, unlike the Zealots for example, Jesus's demands were never backed up by armed force.

Jesus's attitude, therefore, to property and his message that the Reign of God was 'here and now' became the keys to the primitive Christian community's subsequent commitment to the sharing of goods as the most effective, if ultimately unrealistic, way of meeting the day-to-day needs of the whole community of believers, including the poor and helpless. Whilst it had the advantage of being spontaneous it was also said to be non-compulsory, though we should probably be cautious about how voluntary it was in practice. Peer-group pressure based on a shared belief in commonality (*koinonia*) must have been extremely powerful in persuading some of the more reluctant members of the community to toe the line, as is illustrated by the story of Ananias and Sapphira who, having sold their property, attempted to withhold a proportion of the proceeds for their own individual use, and were promptly punished.[5] For people long accustomed to living from hand to mouth this concept of love-communism must have had an enormous appeal for it guaranteed their daily survival, and for the better-off in the group it had all the attraction of dispensing with worldly concerns over possessions. Thus it was the disposal of property and personal holdings that financed the increasingly extensive work of the primitive church, and the apostles who formed the nucleus of community leadership had the responsibility of administering the distribution of the proceeds with the assistance of voluntary workers, as Acts 6.1–6 describes for us, and in a manner that closely paralleled traditional Jewish systems. The Jerusalem Talmud sets out specific arrangements for dealing with poor relief, both on a daily and weekly basis, which the early Christian communities of largely Jewish composition adopted, in order to meet the needs of their own vulnerable co-religionists. Yet again the important point to note here is the continuities that existed between Judaism and primitive Christianity; there was not always a great deal to distinguish the two either in terms of everyday practice or of synagogue worship in the very earliest period after Jesus's earthly life.

Consequently there was a daily distribution of essential foodstuffs initially directed at wandering beggars who, for whatever reason – sickness, disability, dispossession, etc. – had no visible means of support, which very soon became targeted at all poor persons in the community, especially widows and orphans who had nothing to give in return. Relief was always paid out in kind rather than by donations of cash and covered two meal times within a twenty-four-hour period distributed from a central point. For Jerusalem-based Christians this probably took place at the meeting house where they congregated to worship and to share a common meal. Elsewhere in the rural areas of Palestine charitable support was less structured and was organised on a more *ad hoc* basis.

Those requiring support would be offered provisions from gifts that had come in that day to cover their immediate needs for the following day, since food would be difficult to preserve over an extended period of time, especially if the recipients were vagrants; essential items of clothing were a different matter, and again, following Jewish practice, were handed out on a weekly basis. It is likely that included amongst the beneficiaries were the itinerant charismatic preachers who, because of their lack of a settled social existence, were wholly dependent upon local charity to maintain themselves and their wandering lifestyle.

Whether these methods of practical caring and sharing were rural- or city-based they were characterised by the erosion of social distinctions and an acknowledgement that material possessions were of no account in the scheme of priorities but served merely as a means to a common end – the advancement of the Kingdom of God. As a result, in all these affairs there was a conspicuous lack of forward planning – by general consent it was not thought to be necessary – which itself gave rise to difficulties as the Christian mission expanded and the size of the primitive communities grew. In Acts, chapter six, we are given an example of this failure of foresight when widows in the Greek-speaking part of the

Judaeo-Christian community in Jerusalem had been neglected at the time of the daily distribution, a mistake which occasioned dissatisfaction and conflict.[6] However it would be erroneous to think of the Jerusalem community, for all its particular difficulties, as existing in isolation from other groups of believers that were cropping up all over Palestine. The itinerant charismatic preachers were themselves a means of maintaining some level of contact with an expanding network across the country, and when occasion demanded it played a part in the coordination of relief for communities in special hardship by mobilising resources from better-off brethren. The Book of Acts again gives a telling account of how the severe distress experienced by the Jerusalem community during the Claudian famine was handled.[7] The apostles Paul and Barnabas had arrived in the city of Antioch to preach to the community, many of whom were Greek-speaking Jews, and God-fearers and where, we are told, the name 'Christian' was first used. News of the calamity reached the community, which promptly organised such relief as it was able to afford from its communal treasure chest and commissioned the two apostles to deliver it safely. Although circumstances were clearly beyond anyone's control at this time the situation cannot have been helped by the Jerusalem community's lack of interest in planning for the future and setting aside reserves for use in emergencies, thus rendering it vulnerable and consequently dependent on the charity of others – in this case the much better-resourced community in Antioch. But this was all part of the 'love-communism' creed and in the nature of things it was bound to work only in the very short term.

With the rapid development of the Pauline mission and the reluctant acceptance of Gentiles into the ranks of the faithful by the Jerusalem community, the focus soon shifts from the Judaeo-Christian world of Palestine to the Graeco-Roman cities of Asia Minor and the Mediterranean. This change of emphasis reflects both tensions within the homeland communities and the worsening political situation, especially around Jerusalem which had again become a crucible of nationalistic feelings. What had started out in the recent past as an ethically radical renewal movement working amongst a scattered rural population with a core community based in Jerusalem, was now having to come to terms with a membership expanding beyond the borders of Palestine and embracing many different elements, including non-Jews. In such circumstances it is hardly surprising that the innovative shared values of 'love-communism', which after all were the essential marks of radicalism and utterly foreign to traditional social or religious practice, should be found to be inappropriate to the new world of Christian evangelism. Paul and his fellow missionaries were not working with a charismatic, enthusiastic group in the heartland of the Jewish faith. In the urban, Hellenistic communities that were the proving ground of the mission to the Gentiles a wholly different situation obtained.

Expectation of the imminent end of the world was still a powerful theme for Pauline Christianity, but whereas this had led the Jesus movement into radical attitudes towards family and property, in the newly-founded communities outside Palestine there was much more emphasis on mission. Questions about poverty and riches *per se* receive much less attention in the genuine letters of Paul than, say, from the author of Luke-Acts:[8] there is no fundamental criticism of property and wealth and certainly no enthusiasm for having 'all things in common'. On the other hand, social stratification was much more evident and the problems it engendered came quickly into sharper focus.

The particular problems of social division as experienced by a typical Hellenistic Christian community are highlighted by Paul's two epistles to the Corinthians. In his book *The Social Setting of Pauline Christianity*, Gerd Theissen explores the social make-up of the community in Corinth by analysing everything said about it and the difficulties through which it was passing. Paul's concerns are much more about inequality of treatment than the problems of wealth, and Theissen's analysis enables us to accept Paul's starting point that 'not many' in the community belonged to the higher social and economic classes. This is the first telling piece of evidence to suggest that, in Paul's words, there must have been some in the community who were 'wise', 'powerful' and of 'noble birth', thereby contradicting an often-expressed view that early Christianity was a largely proletarian movement.

When we come to a consideration of individuals who are known to us by name through these two letters it is likely that only the most important, and hence those of higher social status, receive a mention; Christians from lower social groups do not generally emerge as significant individuals in the correspondence. Theissen examines offices held, houses occupied in private circumstances, services rendered by specific individuals and journeys undertaken by those of some standing to conclude that there was marked social stratification in the community which became problematic when different groups came together to celebrate semi-ritualistic occasions such as the Lord's Supper. Paul implies that he is disturbed by inconsiderate behaviour on the part of some who attend, bringing their own food with them, more than ample for their needs, and consume it voraciously with no regard for those who are unable so to provide for themselves and consequently go hungry. Not only does such behaviour reveal splits within the community between the 'haves' and the 'have nots' but it leaves unspoken the question of how those in need were to be supported. The clear implication must be that at least on these occasions there should be some sense of sharing and from our knowledge of other similar communities we can be reasonably confident that this is in fact what took place. Furthermore, towards the end of his letter, Paul makes reference to the collection for the 'saints' in Jerusalem, that is for the struggling Christian community there. His suggestion is that each put aside on the Sabbath into the community's treasure chest whatever can be afforded for subsequent onward transmission, and again from this we infer that Paul himself recognised the differing financial circumstances amongst members of the community and the obligation to care for those in need whether at home or 'abroad'.

If Paul has a social message at all, it is one that is clearly set against and even subordinate to his religious message that the Second Coming is imminent and 'our time is growing short' (1 Cor. 7.29). Priority must therefore be given to the task of extending the mission to all corners of the known world and this should involve inculcating in his Hellenistic Gentile converts a quite different sense of social responsibility from the one they had inherited from their pagan backgrounds. The natural circumstances of the new congregations in any case forced this upon them; Paul's claim that predominantly the Gentile Christian communities were poor – in 2 Cor. 8.2 he refers to the intense poverty of the Macedonian churches – does nothing to contradict the fact that most, if not all, congregations contained members of the higher social and economic classes. But Paul's social ethic goes further than this.

In linking salvation theology to social cohesion Paul was effectively dismantling barriers between social classes which had existed from time immemorial in Graeco-Roman society. He tells the Colossians, for example, 'there is no room for distinction between Greek and Jew, between the circumcised or the uncircumcised, or between barbarian and Scythian, slave and free'. His audiences must have been stirred and amazed at such revolutionary preaching that turned long-accepted values on their heads. And if the imminence of the Lord's reappearance gave added urgency to the message at the time, it lost little of its cogency or appeal as eschatological expectations began to fade. In the hostile pagan world of Graeco-Roman society there was little that a struggling new sect could do to change attitudes on a universal level – that would only occur gradually with the advent of Constantine. What could be done, and was indeed achieved, in the Hellenistic Gentile churches of the Pauline mission, was the development of community values, already described above as 'love-patriarchalism', which formed the basis of community care and support. Thus problems of social need were resolved by the Christian community for its own benefit, and this of course presupposed that the necessary means were available to make it possible, provided as always that the will existed to put belief into practice. Again in addressing the church in Corinth Paul sums up what the community's ethical position should be:

> As long as the readiness is there, a man is acceptable with whatever he can afford; never mind what is beyond his

means. This does not mean that to give relief to others you ought to make things difficult for yourselves: it is a question of balancing what happens to be your surplus now against their present need, and one day they may have something to spare that will supply your own need. (2 Cor. 8 12–14)

Documentary evidence for the life and work of the early Church in the immediate post-Pauline period and up to the early second century rests chiefly with the composite work known as the *Didache* or Teaching of the Twelve Apostles. A number of the Apostolic Fathers, whose writings date from the early second century onwards, accorded it the status of Holy Scripture, although the version we possess today was printed in the late nineteenth century from a mid-eleventh-century manuscript discovered at Constantinople and thought to have been much revised over the centuries.[9]

Its date has also been heavily contested, although the weight of current scholarly opinion seems to favour placing its historical locus between AD 70 and 110. It reflects the embryonic church organisation of the late first century by introducing some simple order and structure to the worship of the burgeoning new Christian communities. In common with some other collections of church literature it seems to have evolved by a process of rearranging earlier materials, adding to them and revising. However, its claim to be based on the teaching of the Twelve is an obvious attempt to invest it with apostolic authority in order to commend it as an instruction manual, although there is no reason to doubt that it reflects thinking amongst the Christian leadership of the late first century. Running throughout much early Christian literature there is a strong sense of underlying authority, whether it be apostolic by attribution or simply bearing the name of a visionary church leader with first-hand knowledge of the apostles themselves. Other obvious examples would be the letters to Timothy and Titus attributed to Paul, and the Epistle of Barnabas. For us the value of the *Didache* is in the glimpse it provides of the everyday needs of the Early Church and the ethical basis of its caring work by emphasising how belief is embodied in social forms.

Charity Begins at Home 51

The manual falls into two discernible sections. The first is a moral treatise the basis of which seems to be another work, probably of non-Christian origin (possibly Jewish), entitled 'The Two Ways', setting out the twin paths of life and death. The second gives directions for church rituals and the correct forms for the Lord's Prayer and the Eucharist, concluding with somewhat tendentious advice on how to behave towards missionaries with a final exhortation to watchfulness as against the Lord's second coming. Worthy of note is the fact that this latter part of the manual still makes explicit reference to the itinerant missionaries as they pass from city to city on their evangelising mission. This alone sets at least some of the content at a very early date in the development of the Gentile Christian communities, certainly prior to a more established order of ministry comprising bishops and deacons which characterises the second century.

Because of the importance of the *Didache* as a link between the first generation of Christian apostles and the leading thinkers of the second century, it is worth while quoting the relevant passages that sum up the Church's social thought at this early point of its development. In Part One there is an exhortation to the blessedness of giving which also provides an interesting insight into the plight of the poor Christian community struggling to survive in a pagan society:

> If someone seizes anything belonging to you, do not ask for it back again (you could not get it anyway). Give to everyone that asks, without looking for any repayment, for it is the Father's pleasure that we should share His gracious bounty with all men. A giver who gives freely, as the commandment directs, is blessed; no fault can be found with him. But woe to the taker; for though he cannot be blamed for taking if he was in need, yet if he was not, an account will be required of him as to why he took it, and for what purpose, ... The old saying is in point here: 'Let your alms grow damp with sweat in your hand, until you know who it is you are giving to.'[10]

The significance of not trying to recover one's property highlights the difficulties poor Christians faced to obtain justice before the law which, as always, could prove an extremely costly business. Roman law was able to protect the Roman citizen, but at a price. In the exhortation to giving there are clear echoes of Jesus's teaching, especially in the non-expectation of repayment, and even in the retribution to be exacted from the person who takes unjustifiably when there is no real need. In the last section of Part One there is a further reference made to charitable giving which, interestingly, seems to urge greater generosity than the passage quoted above, and this apparent inconsistency may well reflect the composite nature of the work.

> Do not be like those who reach out to take, but draw back when the time comes for giving. If the labour of your hands has been productive, make an offering as a ransom for your sins. Give without hesitating and without grumbling, and you will see Whose generosity will requite you. Never turn away the needy; share all your possessions with your brother, and do not claim that anything is your own ...[11]

In Part Two of the work, following sections on baptism, fasting and prayer and the eucharist, the author/compiler has included a section on apostles and prophets – or as we might better describe them, missioners and charismatics. In the first of two quotations we find a definite harking back to apostolic times regarding the subsistence required to maintain these two types of evangelist:

> Every missioner who comes to you should be welcomed as the Lord, but he is not to stay more than a day, or two days if it is really necessary. If he stays for three days, he is no genuine missioner. And a missioner at his departure should accept nothing but as much provisions as will last him to his next night's lodgings. If he asks for money, he is not a genuine missioner.[12]

The final quotation continues the subsistence theme as it applies to prophets or charismatic preachers in the congregation.

A genuine charismatist, however, who wishes to make his home with you has a right to a livelihood. (Similarly, a genuine teacher is as much entitled to his keep as a manual labourer.) You are therefore to take the first products of your winepress, your threshing-floor, your oxen and your sheep, and give them as firstfruits to the charismatists, for nowadays it is they who are your 'High Priests'. If there is no charismatist among you, give them to the poor. And when you bake a batch of loaves, take the first of them and give it away, as the commandment directs. Similarly when you broach a jar of wine or oil, take the first portion to give to the charismatists. So, too, with your money, your clothing, and all your possessions; take a tithe of them in whatever way you think best, and make a gift of it, as the commandment bids you.[13]

So far, we have seen how the very earliest communities of Christian believers began to develop informal but clearly laid down systems for the care and support of their own vulnerable co-religionists, based on a restatement of traditional values derived from the mother faith of Judaism. This serves to emphasise the fact that they were, for the main part, Jews or proselytes living amongst Graeco-Roman society and only gradually drawing in Hellenistic Gentiles. To a large extent up to the end of the first century Christianity still remained a deviant movement within a cohesive Jewish culture and although the expanding Pauline mission pushed the boundaries farther and farther away from its native centre, its relationship with other movements in Judaea and in the Diaspora was to remain significant in terms of Christianity's ethical basis. Nevertheless as more and more Gentiles from the Hellenised eastern provinces of the empire and subsequently from the west, including Rome itself, became attracted to the Christian way of life – and indeed increasingly to the Christian way of death – so the communities to which they attached themselves discovered that the moral basis of their belief was to be challenged constantly by the broader culture that confronted them in Graeco-Roman society. Furthermore, as the Christian movement begins to flower, this confrontation reveals both the strengths and strains of a hitherto unimagined universalism.

Notes

1. See Martin Hengel, p. 149, seq., also D. E. Nineham, *Saint Mark*, pp. 269–73.
2. See Martin Hengel, *Was Jesus a Social Revolutionist?* Philadelphia, 1971.
3. For the status of women in the ancient world see, amongst many other scholarly works, *A History of Private Life, from Pagan Rome to Byzantium*, ed. by Paul Veyne and translated by Arthur Goldhammer.
4. Mark 10. 17–27.
5. Acts 5. 1–11.
6. Acts 6. 1–6.
7. Acts 11. 27–30.
8. For a still excellent account of these issues, see Henry Cadbury, *The Making of Luke-Acts*.
9. In 1873 Philotheos Bryennios, head of the Greek school at Constantinople and later Metropolitan of Nicomedia, discovered the manuscript of the *Didache* together with a remarkable collection of documents in the library of the 'Jerusalem Monastery of the Holy Sepulchre' at Constantinople. The collection was bound in one volume and thought to date from the mid-eleventh century. For a list of the works contained in Bryennios's document, see Ante Nicene Fathers, vol. 7, p. 372.
10. *The Teaching of the Twelve Apostles* in Ante Nicene Fathers, vol. 7, chapter 1, 14–20.
11. *Ibid.*, chapter 3, 17–20.
12. *Ibid.*, chapter 12, entire.
13. *Ibid.*, chapter 13, entire.

Chapter Five

Consolidation and Controversy

In the eyes of all Jews and of many Christians (especially those of Jewish birth) the single most cataclysmic event of the second century was the final fall and destruction of Jerusalem in 135. The first serious blow had been dealt sixty-five years previously when the city was severely damaged by Titus, and many of its inhabitants, including Christians, had left for what was, at least in theory, a voluntary exile; now, by virtue of Hadrian's imperial edict, banishment was compulsory for all Jews of whatever persuasion. Jerusalem had effectively been wiped off the map, to be replaced by the new Graeco-Roman city of Aelia Capitolina, the Temple had been destroyed and paganism took root in the soil of Judaism. In the curious way in which things very often happen, the Gentile churches were to benefit from this tragic turn of events. For too long the tensions between Jews and Jewish Christians in Palestine had simmered away, occasionally breaking into open and violent conflict; more seriously for the future of the new faith, the uneasy relationship between the Gentile and Jewish Christian churches had never been fully resolved even after the intervention nearly a century earlier of the Apostolic leaders Peter and Paul. There was a residue of blame on the part of the Gentile churches for the Jews' rejection of Jesus and for their participation in his sufferings and execution; now it seemed as though they had been justly punished, and although Jewish Christians in exile maintained as far as possible many of the traditions of their mother faith, they became increasingly isolated in the Gentile Christian milieu of the second century, and their links with their Judaistic past began to weaken. This could only result in a growing assertiveness on the part of the Gentile communities. The radical renewal movement within Judaism that had been the central feature of Palestinian Christianity was no longer of relevance in the wider Graeco-Roman world; a new spirit was coming into being, a spirit that sought accommodation with the empire on one level but at the same time spawned a different kind of radicalism from which martyrdom was to spring as a new life force. To the world outside the Christian communities, martyrdom was synonymous with fanaticism at worst and eccentricity at best, which is part of the reason why Christianity's appeal to Roman society was ambivalent and remained so throughout the pre-Constantine years.

Although the moral basis of the Christian faith was manifested as much by personal austerity as by demonstrative acts of charity, it nevertheless provided a new direction and its strong spirit of community feeling was acknowledged by Christians and non-Christians alike. There were, however, other aspects of lesser appeal and occasioning grave suspicion. Many of these fell on the apparent exclusivity, perceived to be a distinguishing characteristic of Christian mentality, which asserted the moral high ground over paganism and engendered hostility towards the traditional values of pagan society. Despite this, Christianity made headway as much by the natural expansion of social interchange as by any conscious policy of planned missionary activity. In the wake of Paul's journeys news of the new faith would have been carried along some of the main commercial and military roads by itinerant Christians eager to share their beliefs with curious and sympathetic hearers. Apart from Paul's own correspondence, that generated by Bishop Ignatius of Antioch (d. *c.* 107), a major figure in the post-Apostolic age, itself provides clear evidence of the growth in the numbers of newly established Christian communities, especially throughout Asia Minor. Ignatius' letters are addressed to churches in cities such as Ephesus, Magnesia, Philadelphia, Smyrna and Tralles, strategically situated along important trade routes on the Asian side of the Aegean Sea, as well as much further afield to the church in Rome. And other Christian bishops testify to the expansion of the church in Greece; Polycarp from his see in Smyrna wrote to the church in Philippi and Clement of Rome to the Corinthians. Thus the Church's influence was beginning to have a discernible impact, and throughout the years of imperial tolerance (which vastly outnumbered those of oppression) when the struggles to survive were lessened, the practical application of the principles of Christian community living was to become increasingly embedded in pagan society.

As a result of these developments, as the second century dawns, there is a renewed emphasis on the virtue of almsgiving, especially amongst Christian communities with a significant Jewish heritage where memories of the tithe system derived from Judaism and assimilated by Christianity continued to be cherished. The so-called 'Second Epistle of Clement' of Rome to the Corinthians (not to be attributed to its eponymous author)[1] urges the faithful that 'almsgiving ... is a good thing, even as repentance from sin. Fasting is better than prayer, but almsgiving than both',[2] thereby echoing the views of the genuine Clement in his letter at the end of the previous century to the same Christian community: 'The strong are not to ignore the weak, and the weak are to respect the strong. Rich men should provide for the poor and the poor should thank God for giving them somebody to supply their wants'.[3]

Such moral exhortation was in sharp contrast to that of certain groups whose doctrinal tendencies represented one of the most serious intellectual challenges to orthodox Christian teaching in both early and later church history. Gnosticism, as this system of philosophical thought came to be known, came in a variety of different guises and derived from a syncretism of Platonism, eastern mysticism (especially Zoroastrianism) and elements of Judaism, along with theosophical influences, most of which in one form or another pre-date Christianity. In the course of his missionary activity Paul was confronted by Gnostics at Corinth, where a group considered itself to be spiritually superior to the orthodox community, and at Colossae, where a particularly virulent form of the heresy led the Christian community to believe in intermediate beings in whose hands lay the destiny of mortals, thus outside the reach of Christ's saving grace.[4] The basis of Gnosticism was a dualism which, in oversimplified terms, regarded the spirit as all-important and the body as worthless. To those who embraced this belief care for the physical needs of people was thus anathema, as the Apostolic Father, Ignatius of Antioch, was pungently to point out. 'For love, they have no care, none for the widow, none for the orphan, none for the distressed, none for the prisoner or ex-prisoner, none for the hungry or thirsty.'[5] Gnosticism was to continue to exert a strong influence on the Christian faith but for the more down-to-earth Christian, little interested in what was happening at the intellectual margins, care for the needs of others would remain an obligation to be fulfilled in imitation of Jesus Himself.

By the mid-second century the Church's practical caring work was becoming organised on a more consistent basis, a marked development from a century earlier when charitable giving tended to be *ad hoc* and was evoked as an immediate and spontaneous response to urgent need. The needs were now no less urgent since the communities had mushroomed and moreover frequently insisted on extending assistance to Christians and non-Christians alike, thereby requiring a system to ensure the effective targeting of resources if all obligations to the poor and needy were to be honoured. Assembling together for the purpose of celebrating the Eucharist became the focal point around which almsgiving was centred, with the bishop or presbyters (elders) assuming responsibility both for safekeeping and ultimate distribution, though the latter function was to be delegated to the deacons. Almsgiving covered not only the means of charitable relief but also contributions towards the running expenses of the local church which must have included payments for the maintenance of ministers, who increasingly had no alternative income. Towards the end of the century, during the reign of Commodus, the collection of alms for the poor, and to cover the running costs of the Christian community in Rome, was refined and made notionally more secure by the setting up of a bank deposit in place of the community treasure chest that had been such a feature of the life of the Church since Apostolic times. As can so often be the case with administrative improvements, the new arrangements were destined to cause the church in Rome no small headache.

To what extent similar financial arrangements were able to be made by Christian churches elsewhere is difficult to determine for we have no direct evidence. However, banking and money dealing was a widespread commercial activity throughout the major cities of the empire, and it is likely that other Christian communities took advantage of the facility to obtain interest on money deposited. Bank accounts are certainly known to have existed during the period of the early empire, though the evidence for the later empire is inconclusive. Generally speaking the Roman élite maintained their own safe deposits under personal security at home, and often had a network of contacts available to them for money-lending purposes. Christian leaders would have been concerned about how best to protect the church's assets which in times of persecution were highly vulnerable to seizure by state officials, and even under normal circumstances were susceptible to all the usual vagaries of security, as the Callistus incident (see pp. 95–7 below) illustrates only too well. The demands upon resources not only to meet the daily and weekly needs of the poor, but also to cope with exigences such as famine and war, never lessened, and even prudent forward planning was susceptible to the unexpected; the ransoming of captives is a case in point which Cyprian refers to in his Epistle 59 (see p. 94 below) and seems to have been achieved only by individuals digging deep into their own funds. In the generation following the post-Apostolic age ecclesiastical offices were becoming more clearly defined as the leadership began to lay down demarcation lines for areas of authority and responsibility, in the interests of establishing a mechanism for managing church affairs and of harmonising practice in the Christian communities. There was an increasing need to strengthen local leadership in the face of outbreaks of persecution and, with the rise of heterodoxies such as Gnosticism and Montanism, to safeguard the faithful from exploitation and heresy. Also, for the most vulnerable to know that their future was in competent and caring hands afforded some protection from the depredations of daily life.

Within the radical renewal movement of the first century, the functions of those who ministered to the burgeoning young communities depended on two chief factors, firstly on Apostolic lineage – that is, on knowledge of and contact with the Apostles and their immediate successors, thereby conferring in effect Jesus's own authority upon the community organiser or leader – and secondly on the exercise of special gifts of teaching and prophetic utterance inherited from the itinerant charismatics. Whilst both these types of ministry were still to be found in the Church of the second century and beyond, the Christian world had moved on, and in the astonishingly short space of seventy to a hundred years had developed forms of ministry recognisable in the Holy Orders of today. Paul himself had identified the variety of contributions being made and had attempted to rank them in order of importance: 'first apostles, second prophets, third teachers, next miracle workers, then healers, helpers and administrators.' (1 Cor. 12. 28) No doubt some individuals combined more than one function even in Paul's day, and over the following two or three generations a degree of conflation occurred between some offices so that Ignatius of Antioch, writing in the early second century, could speak of some of the churches of Asia Minor as having a presiding bishop as well as presbyters and deacons.[6] Sometimes bishops and presbyters are spoken of as being of equal rank, as by Clement of Rome in his own letter to the Corinthian church at the time of the persecution under the Emperor Diocletian. The *Didache* (see pp. 50–53 seq. above) of much the same period enjoins Christian communities to 'Appoint for yourselves therefore bishops and deacons worthy of the Lord, men that are meek and not lovers of money, true and reliable; for they also perform for you the ministry of prophets and teachers ....,'[7] perhaps a good example of how functions were beginning to be combined, especially as the itinerant charismatic ministry receded. Differences of function were both practical and liturgical – deacons, for example, not only assisted the bishops or presbyters in celebrating the Eucharist but were involved in the care and administration of church property and of relief to the poor and sick, whilst deaconesses had a duty towards women members of the congregation. The further development in the second century of the bishop's office away from being merely the first presbyter amongst equals to that of a leader with sole authority, and therefore superior to the presbyters, marks the beginning of monarchical episcopacy in the Church and the emergence of the later distinct order of the priesthood.

All these changes reflect the need of the second-century Church to explain and commend itself to the pagan world and at the same time to meet head on the criticisms and distortions of those like the Gnostics and the heretic Marcion who sought to overturn apostolic tradition.[8] A group of writers came to the fore who took it upon themselves to initiate a defence of Christian orthodoxy against such slanders, and thereby represented an important first stage in setting down a systematic account of Christian belief and practice which was to form the basis of future Christian doctrine. The Apologists, as they are known, include some of the Early Church's most distinguished thinkers. Pre-eminent amongst them is Justin Martyr, born in the Samarian city of Flavia Neapolis (anciently called Shechem, the modern city of Nablus) about the turn of the century and brought up as a pagan. His early leanings were to Greek philosophy and he studied with Stoics, Pythagoreans and the disciples of Plato, none of whom, he was convinced, was able to lead him to the truth. As he states himself in his great apologetic work, the *Dialogue with Trypho*, he was then encouraged to study Scripture and from that moment gradually turned to Christianity. The principal works of Justin which have survived may be dated to the middle of the second century, and it is likely that he suffered martyrdom in Rome somewhere between 163 and 167. It is Justin who tells us in *Apology* I: 67 how the local Christian congregation assembles

> on the day which is called the day of the sun to pray and read and to celebrate the Eucharist, at the conclusion of which the deacons take the Eucharistic elements to those unable to be present, presumably through reasons of sickness or imprisonment, whilst the rest of the congregation ... give what they will, each after his choice. What is collected is deposited with the president, who gives aid to the orphans and widows and such as are in want by reason

of sickness or other cause, and to those also that are in prison, and to strangers from abroad; in fact to all that are in need, he is a protector.[9]

In a similar vein the Apologist Aristides, writing about 140, states that Christians do not overlook the widow and do not grieve the orphan. He who has, says Aristides, supplies the needs of him who has not, without grudging. If Christians see a stranger they bring him under their roof and rejoice over him as a real brother.[10] Nor were comments on the quality of care in the Church restricted to Christian writers. Pagan authors, particularly those disposed to be more sympathetic to Christianity and knowledgeable about its affairs, can also be cited as evidence for the Church's practical ministry to those in need. This is important because even by the beginning of the second century the vast majority of the inhabitants of the empire remained largely unaware of the presence of Christianity in their midst. Nor do Christians always emerge covered in credit either for their own actions or those of their co-religionists. The pagan satirist, Lucian of Samosata, reports on the curious business of Peregrinus Proteus, supposedly a Christian from a rather dubious background which included adultery, pederasty and possibly even parricide, who became converted to Christianity in Palestine and soon became a favoured and leading light in the Church which regarded him as a 'new Socrates', such was his expertise in 'the wonderful wisdom of the Christians'. When Peregrinus landed himself in prison for his beliefs he was much visited by his fellow-Christians, some of whom even spent nights with him in his cell, and brought him so many gifts that he began to acquire considerable wealth. Lucian may be guilty of a degree of hyperbole in the telling of his tale, since his disapproval of Peregrinus's behaviour is only too evident, and he wishes to make the point that any smooth talker can take advantage of Christian goodwill. During his spell inside, Peregrinus seems to have more and more donned the garb of a Cynic philosopher so that when he was eventually released through the intervention of the governor of Syria, who was sympathetic to philosophers but also caught on to the fact that the prisoner was something of a publicity-seeker, he resumed his Christian activities but now combined with the role of a Cynic. In a typical gesture of magnanimity he gave his estates to the city of his captivity in gratitude, returned to his native town of Parium and continued to be supported by his fellow-Christians in the style to which he had become accustomed. However, they subsequently threw him out for eating forbidden food, which in one sense is exactly what he had been doing all his life. In a final desperate bid for notoriety he set fire to himself at the Olympic Games in 165.

Lucian's story is significant for two reasons. First of all it illustrates the quite extraordinary lengths to which the Church was prepared to go to support fellow-Christians in trouble, though clearly in Peregrinus's case this went way beyond the meeting of basic needs, and reflects a response to his particular type of persuasive personality which is not without parallel in modern times.[11] Whilst the generosity of the Church was excessive in the circumstances, it nevertheless provides evidence that at this time considerable resources were available when required from the purse of the local Christian community to assist individuals in some kind of difficulty, albeit in this case somewhat undeserving. The source of these funds is likely to have been from a combination of well-off church members acting on their own initiative, and offerings centrally held by the church authorities and collected over a period of time. Even by the second century churches were becoming property-owning organisations with sizeable endowments (and indeed growing commitments), an aspect of Christianity that was to be targeted in successive waves of imperial persecution. In the second place the Church was often viewed by the pagan world as being gullible, easily susceptible to exploitation by ruthless and dishonest persons who by the power of their personalities and their rhetoric were able to seduce church members into parting with considerable sums of money. This is not an entirely unfair view, since Christians clearly provided supporting evidence for it from time to time. Generally speaking, a distinction could be made between the genuine needy person and the fake. Perhaps Peregrinus, whose further appellation of Proteus, after the shape-changing deity, seems highly appropriate, was eventually 'found out' and a means devised for getting rid of him; but in Late Antique society the person of the genuinely holy man was held in reverence and those who followed his teachings would go to almost any lengths both to protect him in the face of perceived injustices, and to minister to his daily needs.

Whilst pagan writers frequently expressed incredulity at the naivety of Christian behaviour, Christian apologists were at pains to demonstrate both the voluntary nature of almsgiving and its moral basis derived from the teaching of Jesus and reinforced by the apostles as, for example, Paul makes clear: '... each one must do as he has made up his mind, not reluctantly or under compulsion, for God loves a cheerful giver.' (2 Cor. 9.7) So Tertullian (c. 160–240), one of the most important Christian apologists of the second/third centuries, in chapter 39 of his *Apology* is quite precise about the church's position on almsgiving and is worth quoting in full.

> Though we have our treasure-chest, it is not made up of purchase-money, as of a religion that has its price. On the monthly day, if he likes, each puts in a small donation; but only if it be his pleasure, and if he is able: for there is no compulsion; all is voluntary. These gifts are, as it were, piety's deposit fund. For they are not taken thence and spent on feasts, and drinking-bouts, and eating-houses, but to support and bury poor people, to supply the wants of boys and girls destitute of means and parents, and of old persons confined now to the house; such, too, as have suffered shipwreck; and if there happens to be any in the mines, or banished to the islands, or shut up in the prisons, for nothing but their fidelity to the cause of God's Church, they become the nurselings of their confession. But it is mainly the deeds of a love so noble that lead many to put a brand upon us. *See*, they say, *how they love one another* ...[12]

A little later in the same chapter the Apologist comments on the Christian attitude towards property. 'So we, who are united in mind and soul, have no hesitation about sharing property. All is common among us except our wives.' We should be careful here not to interpret Tertullian's words as a restatement of the position of the earliest members of the first-century Jesus movement who are known to have held all their worldly possessions in common; in a thoroughgoing sense that had long since passed and in any case had been adhered to relatively briefly. The church of the late second century when Tertullian was writing was very different both in terms of its attitude towards the ownership of property and how it should be managed. The A.N.F. translation given above conveys perhaps a misleading impression, the word used by the Apologist for 'common' – namely, *'indiscreta'* – is better rendered as 'without distinction'. Nevertheless, Tertullian also takes the opportunity to attack in scathing words pagan society's loose behaviour in marriage, but his views should not be assumed to reflect the current norm since, generally speaking, adultery and faithlessness in marriage were not approved of in Graeco-Roman society at large. He is using every weapon in his armoury to illustrate as forcefully as possible the basic differences between pagan and Christian living, and if at times we feel he goes rather over the top it is only to make his readers sit up and take notice. The same approach holds good for his comparisons of Christian meals with pagan feasts. He seems to indicate that the Christian community met together for two distinct types of celebratory meal: the Eucharist, which was an act of thanksgiving for the Life, Death and Resurrection of Christ; and the Agapē, a common meal the occasion of which was specifically designed to provide sustenance for the poor and needy:

> Our dinner shows its idea in its name; it is called by the Greek name for love (*agapē*). Whatever the cost, it is gain to spend in piety's name, for with that refreshment we help the needy ... If the motive of the banquet is honest, take the motive as the standard of the other proceedings required by our rule of life ... Only so much is eaten as satisfies hunger; only so much drunk as meets the needs of the modest.[13]

Tertullian may have been defending Christian practice from pagan criticism but even some pagan writers, like the Platonist Celsus (c. 180) who was not above accusing Christians of sorcery, allow the cohesiveness of Christian communities as distinct groups within society, which they attribute, perhaps over-simplistically, to the Christian experience of persecution. At any rate, this is a sign that the pagan world was beginning to recognise that the Church possessed the potential at least to influence, if not radically to alter, the prevailing social order. Tertullian is citing pagan opinion when he reports the view that Christians' love for one another is worthy of note. Many of the Christian writings of the second century, including those quoted above, adopt an unequivocal moral stance which undoubtedly carried some resonance for Graeco-Roman society at large.

Following the deaths of Marcus Aurelius in 180 and eleven years earlier of his co-emperor and son-in-law, Lucius Verus, both of natural causes, his son Commodus, the last of the Antonines, who had also been co-emperor with his father since 177, was assassinated after a reign of fifteen years as the result of a palace plot. Each of the next four emperors suffered violent deaths within a space of four years, before the Severan dynasty came to power in the final years of the century. Confidence in the political system was shaken if not seriously undermined. Economically, too, the empire's affairs were in a downward spiral which, by the time of Diocletian, was to reach a crisis.[14] Against such a background of instability and nervousness about what the future might bring, the forces of reaction are wont to assert themselves as people seek refuge in the security of past certainties. It is not surprising, therefore, to discover that the late second century is characterised by an almost obsessive entrenchment in traditional values and established social norms. The age of the Antonines had started to slide into political decline with the reign of the young, unstable and anti-traditionalist Commodus, probably his father's reluctant choice as a successor, anxious as Marcus Aurelius was to avoid the possibility of a civil war over the throne after his death. The consequent upheavals preceding the accession of Septimius Severus gave an added impetus to a process that had been under way throughout the second century, of the revitalisation of the empire's cultural heritage. In towns and cities across the empire the wealthy élite were expending vast sums on both secular and religious public works, and imperial patronage was supporting to a considerable extent those ambitions of municipal and provincial status eagerly sought by the rich minority. Divisions in society were thus widening as wealth was concentrated in the hands of the few, with minor provincial officials becoming a new class of poor and the existing hard-pressed poor, both in the countryside and the towns, sliding further into debt and destitution. Imperial government was not wholly insensible to these problems, merely unwilling and unable to prescribe effective remedies.

If the Church was acquiring a well-deserved reputation for caring for its own, then the Roman state could at least protest, with a degree of justification, that it had been trying to do just that for rather longer. As early as the second century BC there is evidence that the Roman authorities sanctioned distributions of grain for the populace of the city, known as *frumentum* or grain dole. The numbers of those in receipt of this benefit rose and fell significantly under various regimes, and classical commentators are by no means unanimous on the matter of who qualified, though the weight of opinion seems to favour the view that Roman citizenship, rather than actual proof of need, alone led to entitlement. From the time of the empire onwards the distribution was no longer confined to the city of Rome but also took place in other urban centres in the provinces and, as conditions for the lower classes deteriorated, it became an important means of sustaining a population under economic and political stress. Between the second and third centuries AD up to 100,000 people in Rome and its surrounding districts were said to be in receipt of the dole; this is almost certainly a conservative estimate, especially as we have no means of knowing how many of these were actually below the poverty line. A major contributory factor to the overall economic situation was the increasing militarisation of the empire and the burden upon the state of paying, indeed doubling pay, and provisioning a vast army now becoming heavily involved in large-scale mercenary recruitment. It has been estimated that during the course of the third century the Roman army rose to something in excess of 350,000 fighting men. Partly because of the lack of hard cash (as inflation took off, the currency obviously devalued) payments were as often as not made in kind, thus imposing a devastating burden upon the civilian population. With a rising death rate amongst the rural poor, and generous grants of land throughout the empire required to pay off retiring veterans, agricultural production was severely depressed, especially so in Italy. The Romans had no understanding of crop rotation and it is thought that as much as 15 per cent of land across the empire as a whole was going to waste annually, though not necessarily all of this would have been in prime farming areas. Added to these problems was the attitude of the soldiers; understandably frustrated by years of working for little and sometimes no pay, and discovering that rampant inflation was eroding whatever they had, they turned against the very people least culpable for their plight, and terrorised local communities with menaces and worse in order to obtain the supplies they required. Appeals for intervention made to successive emperors fell mostly on deaf ears and anyway there was little they could do to control such widespread abuses, which involved officers as well as men. As the demand for food went on increasing, rural communities had to suffer in silence and produce whatever they could to satisfy the all-consuming state.

Christianity, with its moral mandate to care for disadvantaged people whether its own or not, and preaching essentially a message of deliverance from the ills of this world, was well placed to attract the interest of those who felt they had most to gain from the Church's strong sense of solidarity and inclusiveness, and its advocacy, at least in theory, of the principle of egalitarianism; a broad spectrum of society is thus represented, from the disadvantaged poor to the disenchanted well-off. Although still very much a minority sect the Church was able to make inroads across the empire as a whole and especially in those parts where Roman rule was not so long established and where, therefore, the traditional structures were of more recent provenance and more fragile. Here and elsewhere the Church was able to offer the opportunity of living in a form of community within the secular world which could provide a focus for those who no longer felt at ease in pagan circles, and which could afford some protection from the worst excesses of social and economic circumstances, even though this led to charges of exploiting the fears of the poor. In many ways the Church expanded precisely because it was able to trade on the anxieties of the age. There were some Christians, of course, who thought that spiritually the poor were better off as they were free from the temptations of Mammon, though these voices are unlikely to have come from the ranks of the unemployed and hungry.

Defining the nature of communal life was for the Church a dynamic process that had to be worked out experientially, during the course of which issues about authority, status, wealth and behaviour continued to be at the forefront of debate, much as they had been in St Paul's day, but now overlaid with the added complexities of a property-owning organisation presided over by a monarchical episcopacy. A snapshot of one such community wrestling with these questions in the first half of the second century has been provided by the Christian slave writer Hermas,[15] written in the form of a series of visions said to have been revealed to him in and around the city of Rome, which is thus intended to be the locus where the resolution of these difficulties should take place. Although Rome was the largest Christian enclave of the time, it is a typical enough setting of urban Christianity to serve as an appropriate illustration of how the Church was trying to grapple with current problems of community living. The title of the work, *The Shepherd*, refers to the figure of a divine teacher who, by use of Visions, Mandates and Similitudes, instructs Hermas in moral lessons which are further to be imparted by him to the Roman church. Concerns had abounded about the use to which some members were putting their wealth, and this in turn raised questions about the relative status of rich and poor. Hermas, the former slave of a Roman lady called Rhoda, towards whom he had at one time felt more than would normally be expected between slave and mistress of the house, had clearly done well for himself and achieved a position of influence amongst the

Christian community – sufficient, at any rate, for him to be regarded as a credible mouthpiece of the Lord. His own view of life was simple and straightforward, and he was uncomfortable with a situation where the Roman church was being supported by rich benefactors whose preoccupation with maintaining their secular business interests for the benefit of their families seemed at variance with their responsibilities as members of the church, thus rendering their position in the community ambiguous.

In Similitude Two of the work,[16] the parable of the rich man and the poor man makes clear that each is expected to complement the other and that each has a role to play in upholding the faith and solidarity of the community. Earlier, in Vision Three, Hermas warns the rich that failing to share with the poor can only result in harm to themselves; they get sick with overeating, he says (a common complaint amongst the Roman upper classes), whilst others suffer because of hunger. Hermas is describing normal daily behaviour in the Roman world which would have passed without notice in secular society, but the Church has already prescribed a different standard for its baptised members and this is being blatantly ignored. Almsgiving, too, is emphasised as important in Mandate Two:[17] '... give to all who are in need fairly, not questioning to whom you shall give. Give to all ... He then who gives is guiltless ... making no distinction ...' But the community is also experiencing deeper problems, perhaps arising from these inequalities and from the double standards being applied by the better off, for slander and evil speaking has taken hold and there is a need for the community to return to a purer way of life. 'Maintain simplicity and be guileless, and you shall be as little children who do not know the wickedness which can destroy their lives. First of all, speak evil of no man, neither take pleasure in listening to a slander ... slander is evil; it is a restless demon, never at peace but always at home among factions.'[18]

It is in passages such as these, which recur throughout the writings of Early Church leaders and thinkers, that we are given a glimpse of the moral struggles to keep the faithful united and uncontaminated by the standards of a pagan society, of which the Church was at one and the same time both an inextricable part and yet uniquely different. Moral confusion was an inevitable concomitant for a group which never intended or desired to withdraw from society, as had been the case with the early charismatic movements in rural Palestine, but whose hope and aim was to become an accepted and increasingly influential part of that society. Ambivalence on the part of some grass-roots members was bound to be a feature of a community's continued existence, especially when faced with a leadership that was trying to change attitudes about responsibility to one another which were, by and large, not embraced by wider Roman society, and at the same time accepting that basic social divisions would remain. If the Roman world of the second century was pervaded by deeply traditionalist mores, the fact remains that the social habits of the Christian communities were a reflection of the same values and were generally rather conservative too, with a marked tendency to concur with the *status quo* in the largely justified belief, that there was little that could be done to address the divisions in society, and in particular the widening gulf between the rich minority and the remaining bulk of the population. A fundamental questioning of the social order as such consequently did not arise and even the Christian communities themselves mirrored and perpetuated normal class divisions. Hermas was not proposing radical social change when he urged the Roman community to brush up on its manners, but neither was he ignoring the fact that certain aspects of commercial activity involved a moral dilemma between the demands of economic prudence and those of religious obligation.

Although cohesiveness acted as the Church's counterbalance to the secular world, there was to be another aspect of religious life of even greater significance which came to dominate Late Antiquity, and that was the rise to prominence of the person of the holy man of God. A shift of focus takes place in religious thinking and practice over the ensuing hundred years following the accession of Septimius Severus, which was to put the Christian Church of the fourth century at the very centre of the map of Mediterranean life, with the resultant displacement of the ancient civic role of the Graeco-Roman city. Change was gradual but ineluctable, and yet was not to be accomplished without struggle and bloodshed. The second century and the age of the Antonines in particular furnished conditions which enabled the Church to establish itself at the margins of Roman life and to begin a learning process about understanding and coping with complex human issues. All the Church's resources, personal and material, would be put thoroughly to the test in the changing fortunes of the third century, when, more than in any previous time, periods of imperial tolerance – or, at the very least, official disregard – would be punctuated by instances of vicious imperial persecution. How the Church survived and embedded itself even deeper in Graeco-Roman society will be the subject of chapter Six.

Notes

1. This was one of two epistles attributed to St Clement of Rome which were discovered by Bryennios and published in 1875. See note 9 of chapter 4 above.
2. *Second Epistle of Clement*, chapter 16 in Ante Nicene Fathers, vol. 7.
3. *First* (genuine) *Epistle of Clement*, chapter 38 in Ante Nicene Fathers, vol. 1. Translation quoted here is from *Early Christian Writings*, translated by Maxwell Staniforth.
4. See Henry Chadwick, *The Early Church* (Pelican History of the Church) p. 33 seq.
5. See *Ignatius of Antioch, Epistle to the Smyrneans*, shorter version, in Ante Nicene Fathers, vol. 1.
6. Several of Ignatius's genuine letters to the churches of Asia Minor refer to the office of 'bishop', e.g. Ephesians, Magnesians, Trallians, Philadelphians and Smyrnaeans.
7. See *The Teaching of the Twelve Apostles (The Didache)*, chapter 15, Ante Nicene Fathers, vol. 7.
8. Marcion, a Christian from Asia Minor, is associated with the Gnostics but his system of thought is also quite distinct. He was excommunicated as a heretic in 144. See further Henry Chadwick, op. cit., pp. 38–40.
9. See the works of *Justin Martyr* (110–c. 165), in Ante Nicene Fathers, vol. 1, p. 159 seq.
10. See *Aristides of Athens* (c. 125–145), Ante Nicene Fathers, vol. 9, p. 263 seq.
11. The problem is one that has recurred throughout Christian history. Some unscrupulous television evangelists in America and elsewhere would be cases in point.

12. See Tertullian, *Apology*, chapter 39, Ante Nicene Fathers, vol. 3, p. 46.
13. Tertullian, above, p. 181.
14. Recommended further reading on this subject, and for a somewhat different view, see two works by Averil Cameron, *The Later Roman Empire* and *The Mediterranean World in Late Antiquity*. Professor Cameron's views on the late Roman economy, along with her cautious approach to traditional presentations on 'decline and fall' need to be taken seriously. See note 13 of chapter 6, below.
15. See *The Shepherd* of Hermas (*c*. AD 90–150), Ante Nicene Fathers, vol. 2, p. 9 seq.
16. *Ibid.*, p. 32.
17. *Ibid.*, p. 20.
18. *Ibid.*, p. 20.

Chapter Six

Changing Fortunes

The advent of the Severan dynasty in the closing years of the second century heralded an unprecedented and unexpected period of changing fortunes for the Christian Church.[1] These fortunes were linked by both cause and effect to a remarkable shift in the patterns of social life in the cities and towns of the Mediterranean. For centuries this had been a 'small-town'-minded society, locally controlled by social élites in relationships of interdependence from which municipal and personal prestige blossomed to the benefit of all save the most disadvantaged. Such of these as happened to be Christian, and even some who were not, were partially protected by the charity of the local Christian community. The Mediterranean, however, was no longer just *mare nostrum*, 'our sea', it was part of a greatly expanded Roman world and one where the strains of distant conquest were beginning to tell. The central administration of the empire's affairs, despite a growing bureaucracy and enlarged civil service, was no longer able to cope; the army was over-stretched and irregularly paid and the precarious rural economy bore the brunt, to its own detriment, of supporting the urban populations. It was also a world of increasingly marked social contrasts. Lavishness in the provision of local amenities was matched only by the deprivations of the lowest social classes; even during the heyday of the Antonines we are told that the doctor Galen from Asia Minor noted the symptoms of widespread malnutrition and, with rising prices and the rapid devaluation of the currency, matters had got progressively worse.[2]

On the borders of the empire new concentrations of power threatened the already tenuous hold the Romans exercised over their remoter territories. For so long a threat to Rome's eastern border, the troublesome Parthians had been slipping into decline, and in 224 the Sassanid dynasty in Persia took over control of the country and annexed former Parthian lands, soon making it clear that Rome could no longer assume its right to dominance over the region. Shapur I, King of Kings, quickly demonstrated the superiority of his armoured cavalry in attacks launched against the Romans in 252 and 257, culminating in the ignominious capture of the Emperor Valerian in 260 and the seizure of Antioch. To the north, the Goths of the Danube basin formed a loose confederacy in 248, and in 251 slew the Emperor Decius and much of his army. By 270 every one of the empire's borders had yielded to external threat and crumbled. Following the assassination by mutinous troops in 235 of the last Severan, Alexander, the ruling dynasty had come to an end after a mere forty-two years, with only one of its members dying in his bed of natural causes. Thereafter Rome entered an age of military anarchy. No fewer than thirty-four emperors were proclaimed by the armies over the forty-nine years between 235 and the accession of Diocletian in 284 and, again, of these only three suffered non-violent ends, although the little-known Carus is rumoured to have been struck by lightning after a typically short reign of ten months, an explanation almost certainly euphemistic. Barbarian incursion increased along the Rhine and Danube rivers, and the coasts of Britain and Gaul were subjected to the ravages of raiding parties with a ferocity that reminds us of the Viking age to come. As frontier posts became deserted when the legions pulled back or were overrun, military commanders set up secessionist empires to try and introduce a degree of local stability, recognising that Rome had now placed an impossible distance between itself and its outlying provinces and gambling that it was the right moment to sever ties, although there is little doubt that personal ambition played as prominent a part as political altruism in these enterprises. Between 260 and 268 Britain, Gaul and Spain temporarily broke away, and in the east the formidable and erudite Zenobia, the widow and successor of Odenathus, ruled over the Empire of Palmyra for three hectic years from 267. During this time she extended Palmyrene power throughout Asia Minor and even managed to seize Egypt, evidently a source of immense satisfaction as she had always admired Cleopatra. Declaring her son Augustus and herself Augusta, in emulation of Roman imperial style, she was subsequently defeated in battle by the Emperor Aurelian who had set out to recover the empire's lost eastern territories, and her final appearance on the stage of history was a starring role in Aurelian's Triumph clad, symbolically and glamorously, in golden chains and adorned in jewels, after which she faced a comfortable and peaceful retirement in exile in Tivoli. This colourful and energetic woman provides one of the most notable examples in Late Antiquity of outstanding female leadership.

At the height of the military crisis in the third century the Roman world must have seemed to be falling apart, yet paradoxically these events account for an important development in the conduct of Roman military affairs.[3] Any appraisal of the army's effectiveness highlights the need for radical reform, and it was clear that this should permeate from top to bottom. A professional officer class of men who had risen from the ranks through merit, assumed the most senior commands which had hitherto been conferred as of birthright on the senatorial class. From 260 onwards senators were specifically excluded: soldiering was henceforth to be an occupation for professionals, the rewards for which could bring high office in the state, up to and including the imperial purple itself. The resulting changes produced a beneficial counterbalance to the empire's military problems. Although becoming increasingly 'barbarian' in composition through mercenary recruitment, the reconstituted army was now more broadly based, especially after Caracalla granted Roman citizenship to all inhabitants of the empire, and army service, which had tended to become hereditary, carried enormous benefits in land, goods and greatly enhanced pay. Campaigns launched by Gallienus in 258 and again in 260 against foreign incursion in north Italy and the Balkans marked the turning of the tide in the west, to be echoed in the east in 296 when Galerius repulsed the encroaching Persians. Under new commanders of genius the empire gradually regained control over its own frontiers, and this reversal of fortune is one of the outstanding achievements of the Late Antique period. But the cost in terms of life, property and money was incalculable.

Civilians in the old heartlands of the empire were, for the most part, less interested in the outcomes of foreign policy or military reform – or for that matter in the frequent and violent changes of leadership, which impinged very little on their lives. Of more urgent concern were the problems of their local economy. The persistent demands of the taxman concentrated minds on the priorities of daily living, and the state's mounting requirements for money and goods in kind to support an army doubling in size and embarked on distant and risky ventures, were themselves reasons enough for widespread anxiety.[4] In Mediterranean terms the *Pax Romana* was still perceived to be a reality and there was no enthusiasm for skirmishing on far-flung borders which meant little to the ordinary citizen; the concept of the Roman world as a 'global village' was totally unknown; small towns meant small horizons, and it seemed unfair and repressive to the people that they should have to bear the heaviest share of the burden of keeping the empire together.

Inevitably the burden fell doubly hard on the members of Christian communities. Not only were they required to fulfil all the normal obligations of a taxpaying citizen, but they also had to face up to the added problems of trying to maintain their charitable commitments to the Church's treasure chest for the relief of the poor and needy, whose plight was greatly exacerbated by the economic hardship from which the Empire was suffering, with consequent heavy demands upon limited resources.

Yet despite these decades of upheaval it is a tribute to the ancient solidarity of the Mediterranean communities that the fabric of everyday life remained as firm as it did while the civilian population gritted its teeth and held on. Sheer stoic determination enabled Graeco-Roman society to survive the economic crisis of the third century and to accommodate the gradual transformation of traditional social structures which occurred as the Christian Church increased its influence at every level at the expense of paganism and integrated itself

78   *The Treasure Chest of the Early Christians*

with community life. Its promise of salvation in the name of Jesus, and its growing reputation for being a socially concerned movement appealed to people who were becoming increasingly aware of the weakness of Roman imperium and the silence of the gods. A resurgence of interest in paganism which flowered briefly amongst philosophical thinkers in the late second century did not extend to the majority, nor was it able to be sustained for long. Although it represented an attempt at a genuine intellectual revival, the climate was against it. The pantheon of ancient gods seemed in terminal decline as worship was neglected and temples were abandoned. In later years the intellectual Emperor Julian, known as the Apostate, who tried to reintroduce official pagan cults, attributed the disrepute into which they had fallen to the miseries of war which 'led people to despise the gods'.[5] This was not, however, the whole truth.

From the age of the Antonines onwards there had been a gradual coalescence of the pagan deities who initially appear as representatives of a supreme divine being or chief god and develop into distinct attributes or aspects of the divinity.[6] This is a period in which a new sense of spirituality is awakened against a background of national turmoil. Although paganism was losing ground it remained at the centre of the Graeco-Roman psyche, embodying the spirit of places, such as Eternal Rome, of virtues such as patriotism and loyalty, and even of the persons of the emperors themselves. True, many of the ancient festivals of the gods had degenerated into mere opportunities for public celebration but nevertheless Genius, which was the essence of the gods' divinity, was still believed to be encapsulated in the Roman people and ultimately in their rulers. At the same time the divine being in a variety of forms came to be identified as the companion and protector of the emperor, and successive rulers chose a particular god or divine attribute under whose aegis they would achieve victory over their enemies and fulfil their destiny. The Roman world was slowly drifting towards monotheism. Under the Severans, especially Septimius and his great-nephew the Syrian-born Elagabalus, the belief in a single deity centred on the worship of the Sun-

God, which began to assume a pre-eminent place in religious thinking. Sun-worship had from earliest recorded times been a dominant feature in ancient religions; the Old Testament makes reference to the forthcoming Messiah as the 'Sun of Righteousness' and similar imagery occurs constantly throughout the Middle East from Egypt to Asia Minor and Persia. When Constantine first adopted the Sun-God as his protector he was both following familial tradition and also recognising that the cult had long established itself amongst his Balkan ancestors. Closely linked to sun-worship but taking it to a much deeper level for the individual cultist was the centuries-old Persian religion of Mithraism, the origins of which can be traced to the sixth century BC and which spread westwards across Asia Minor and into eastern Europe, acquiring many accretions along the way and being found extensively amongst the Roman populations of Gaul and Britain. The attraction of Mithraism, as with Christianity, was the fact that it was a salvation religion but with the essential difference that it rested on a dualism of good and evil, something it shared with many other ancient religious traditions, such as Gnosticism and Manichaeism, and which was deeply embedded in Graeco-Roman philosophical thinking. Orthodox Christianity had firmly set its face against any form of dualistic belief, and Mithraism was destined to fail in its appeal where the Church succeeded, although historians are probably less confident about the precise reasons for this than once appeared to be the case.

Nevertheless, the Church ultimately triumphed and even managed to ride out some vicious episodes of persecution in the course of the third century. Hitherto persecution had mainly, but not exclusively, been a response to rather local concerns on the parts of provincial governors or over-zealous magistrates to Christian assertiveness, arising from proselytism or determined opposition to the cult of emperor-worship. A notable exception was the outbreak of violence that occurred in AD 64 in Nero's reign after a great fire swept through a large part of the city of Rome, destroying many buildings and extensively damaging others. Nero himself may well have been personally responsible for the conflagration, even if not actually igniting it, in which case it was hardly surprising that he should look around for someone else to blame. Christians became the scapegoats and many lost their lives by being crucified and then used as human torches.[7] Persecution continued sporadically over the next two centuries, with the Church working hard to strengthen the waverers and to contain the excessive enthusiasm of those a little too eager to acquire the martyr's crown. However, persistent attempts to suppress Christianity had on the whole a positive effect upon the morale of local congregations, as seems evident from the steady but undeniably modest numbers of converts throughout the period, which latter fact probably explains why some secular commentators failed to register awareness of the presence of the Church in their midst. Numerically, Christianity was to remain a minority cult for a considerable time to come, and members of the Church, particularly those born into the upper echelons of Roman society, were acutely conscious of their doubtful standing in the eyes of their fellow citizens. A sense of social insecurity bound them together with a cohesiveness that would stand them in good stead when fortune turned against them and their resolution was put to the test. That moment was about to be realised on some spectacular occasions during the third century as attacks were launched on the Church at the personal instigation of the emperor himself. Perhaps at those times when external threats to the empire's security temporarily receded Christians tended to be viewed as the 'enemy within', especially as loyalty inside the armed services was becoming an issue of concern, for which the Church stood accused of being partly responsible by dividing allegiance between Christ and the state.

It is now thought by some scholars of the period that the supposed edict of Septimius Severus against Christian proselytism, recounted by Eusebius of Caesarea in his *History of the Church*, as well as by other writers, cannot be substantiated from contemporary sources and that therefore the persecutions in Alexandria and Africa during Septimius's reign were again locally inspired.[8] Not all those who lost their lives were catechumens, in fact the father of Origen, the elderly Leonidas, a baptised Christian of many years standing, was martyred at this time. But despite difficulties of this kind there were also intervals of respite, during one of which Origen was able to start up his school again, before resentment once more returned. News of these moves against the Church circulated rapidly throughout the eastern half of the empire, alarming Christian communities everywhere and assuming the proportions of a general imperial rescript. All the evidence suggests, however, that Christianity enjoyed a remarkable degree of tolerance under the Severan emperors, although Septimius is wrongly thought to have displayed hostility towards the Jews, and this reputation may have been mistaken in the minds of some for anti-Christian feeling. Under Elagabalus and his cousin and successor, Alexander, the Church was allowed to flourish unmolested; Alexander is known to have had a number of Christians in his household and even among members of his family. His assassination at the hands of the army in 235 brought a Thracian to the throne. Maximinus was proclaimed by his predecessor's killers, and the ensuing persecution of Christians ascribed to him is again disputed in terms of its scale. Eusebius, backed up by other sources, tells us that it derived from the new emperor's 'resentment' of Alexander and his House which was 'made up for the most part of Christians'[9] a typically Eusebian exaggeration that nevertheless contained a grain of truth.

One of the most serious and prolonged waves of persecution occurred at the outset of the reign of Decius (249–51).[10] Sacrificing to the gods was now the issue at stake, and this time it was not only the direct intervention of the emperor himself that made matters so grave but also the application of the edict throughout the empire. All citizens were forced to demonstrate their loyalty by duly sacrificing before specially-appointed commissioners and thereupon to receive written proof of having done so. Those who refused were dealt with accordingly, and the Church took an equally strong line with those who cheated by trying to buy their way out. Inevitably such action on the part of the secular authorities caused some church leaders to go underground and thereby to earn the lasting scorn of those who were imprisoned for their faith. Decius' edict was clearly aimed at reasserting the authority of the pagan gods, in reaction to the encouragement Christianity had received from his predecessor Philip the Arab, who was thought by some to have himself embraced the faith and to have made an act of public penance for the death of Gordian.

The Valerian persecution pressed Decius' policy a stage further by targeting the Church itself as a recognised institution within the empire.[11] Church activity was hindered by the prohibition of the right of assembly for worship, and Christians who had obtained official positions within the state bureaucracy were especially vulnerable. One of the most noticeable effects of this prohibition, although relatively short-lived, was the difficulty Christian communities experienced in organising the continued collections of alms and their subsequent distribution. Where local bank deposit arrangements existed, as for instance in Rome, it is reasonable to suppose that the churches would have had to allow for the fact that reduced rates of interest would have further depleted the value of the accumulated resources of the treasure-chest. In times of centrally-instigated repression, having responsibility for safeguarding and investing the Church's monies would be regarded as a particularly risky undertaking. Under such pressures capital tends to be utilised and diminishes rapidly; if it cannot easily or quickly be replaced then a serious financial situation looms and there may have to be a disposal of other assets. On this occasion there is no suggestion that matters went so far, unlike the results of the later Diocletian persecution, recounted below, when church assets were themselves the special target of the commissioners. Nevertheless, the prohibition was in itself a *de facto* acceptance that the Christian Church was becoming a significant influence within the empire, otherwise there would have been little point of a rescript of universal application. But Valerian's capture by the Persian king brought an end to his strictures against the Church, and his son and successor, Gallienus, completely reversed his father's policy, partly because of his opposition to the dyed-in-the-wool pagan-minded senate. An edict of tolerance was declared which became, in effect, the first formal recognition of the Church's right to exist; furthermore, Gallienus took it upon himself to ensure that not only were the empire's magistrates acquainted with his decision, but the bishops were also made aware so that they, too, could take steps locally to see that the members of their flocks were protected. Forty years of calm ensued for the Church – a calm that was the prelude to a much greater storm than anything that preceded it. Much ground required to be made up by strengthening the Church's dwindled resources and coping with the increased numbers of persons who, as has been suggested, had suffered as a result of the enforced cutback in charitable activity. Despite all its vicissitudes the Church had survived for over two and a half centuries and consolidated its position; it had addressed, and continued to do so, questions of faith and order, wrestled with the often intractable problems of orthodox and heretical belief and produced some of the most towering personalities ever to be spread across the canvas of its history. Furthermore, it had set a unique standard of practical caring for vulnerable members of the community. But all this achievement was soon to be thrown into jeopardy by the one occupant of the imperial throne who avowedly did more to reform and shore up the infrastructure of the empire than any of his predecessors since Augustus established the Principate, although, despite this, the Empire's economic problems were destined to continue in the same vein well into the reign of Constantine.

Caius Aurelius Valerius Diocletianus, known to history as the Emperor Diocletian, was born in Dalmatia about the year 245. He succeeded to the hegemony of the Roman Empire in 284 following the death of Numerian. From all that has been said, it is clear that he inherited an empire in crisis. Lack of political continuity and stability had weakened all the major institutions to the point where the economic health of the state seemed about to disintegrate and the sheer cost of national defence had escalated out of proportion to the population's ability to sustain it. There was a serious lack of gold and silver resources in the government's coffers and, indeed, the silver currency, most commonly used in many day-to-day transactions, had collapsed. In order to tackle the complex problems of reconstruction Diocletian divided the empire into eastern and western parts and appointed a fellow

Augustus, the co-emperor Maximian, to govern in the west. Under the new arrangements each of the two Augusti was to be assisted by a Caesar – Galerius in the east and Constantius Chlorus, the father of Constantine the Great, in the west. Thus, the Tetrarchy came into existence as a political innovation that survived barely two decades. Measures designed to reform fiscal policy, to stabilise the debased currency and to put taxation on to a more rational level by improving the means of its collection (which in practice exacerbated the difficulties people were already in), followed the political reorganisation in an attempt to stem the crisis.[14] The specific effects of Diocletian's economic policy upon the Christian Church are difficult to quantify, since documentary and archaeological evidence is in short supply. Clearly, more efficient tax collection must have involved a reduction in the disposable income to which people had become accustomed, and it is impossible to imagine that this did not have at least some knock-on effect upon the level of charitable giving, with a resulting further erosion of the Church's resources and its ability to continue to care for the poorest in the community. So yet again, in a little over thirty years, a financial crisis put pressure upon Christians at a time when the need for community care was greater than ever. And these problems only paved the way for worse to come. On the other hand, Christians had shown on many occasions in the past that they could be determined and unwavering in carrying on with the Lord's work in the face of considerable odds. The youthful Origen, for example, had been so fired up by the arrest and subsequent execution of his father, that, far from running from danger, his mother had barely restrained him from following suit. He went on in his eighteenth year to take charge of the catechetical school in Alexandria, at that time without a head, devoting himself to the task of instructing others in the faith. Certainly he was fortunate in having found a wealthy patroness to back him, since after his father's death the family had been left in poverty; doubtless there were many others who found themselves in much less favourable circumstances. Dionysius, Bishop of Alexandria, in an epistle quoted by Eusebius (*Eccl. Hist.* Bk. 7 ch. 22) refers to the 'pestilential disease' which fell upon the city following the

Valerian persecution and hard upon the heels of the war with Persia. 'The most of our brethren,' he writes, 'were unsparing in their exceeding love and brotherly kindness.' Many of them, Dionysius tells us, sacrificed their own lives in nursing the sick. Doubtless some communities responded better than others, depending on the quality of local leadership provided by their bishops and clergy: if the evidence of the Diocletian persecution is anything to go by, the Church was far from united in its approach to crisis situations.

Fundamental to Diocletian's reconstruction was the restoration of the empire's most ancient traditions, and these included the reinstatement of the Roman gods and of their temple rites. Paganism had been struggling to survive against the monotheistic tendencies of the Severan dynasty and more recently that of Gallienus, and this had created a climate of tolerance from which the Church had benefited. Monotheism, in reality, was finding expression in a move towards religious syncretism centred on the cult of the Sun-God, which was evolving into the concept of a *summus deus*, a supreme god of many names and attributes, into which the God of the Christians could, at least in non-Christian eyes, be fitted. The return of the pagan gods was intended to arrest this trend and was thus bound to shatter the Church's peace. Confrontation was slow in coming; the first signs that the tide was turning against the Christians arose twelve years into Diocletian's reign, and the influence of Galerius on the emperor at this time is not without significance. According to the admittedly hostile Christian writer, Lactantius,[15] although Diocletian was initially cautious in his handling of the situation and wished to avoid violence, Galerius increasingly played on his pagan susceptibilities and whipped up his anger against the Church.[16] Diocletian was aware of the implications of proceeding too vigorously against an influential minority which had already infiltrated every aspect of national life and been treated to a remarkable degree of acceptance, but he was not prepared to allow it to interfere with his overall plan for the rejuvenation of the empire according to long-established ideals. The full force of the storm at its height was so ferocious and the damage to the Church so extensive that it has become known to history as the Great Persecution.

But there were other forces at work as well. Neo-Platonists, led by the philosopher Plotinus and his disciple and biographer Porphyry,[17] were also making a comeback and, encouraged by a renewed interest in Hellenistic thought, were seeking to stimulate an intellectual revival at the expense of Christianity. Porphyry had produced a virulent *magnum opus* attacking the Church, entitled *Against the Christians*, which was enthusiastically taken up by his colleague, Hierocles, the neo-Platonist governor of Bithynia. Under the latter's influence Galerius was urging that Christians in the armed services should be required to reaffirm their loyalty to the state by being forced to sacrifice to the gods. Although loyalty in the army was becoming an issue of concern, there had never been any doubt that Christians discharged faithfully their full obligations as members of a fighting force and, perhaps in recognition of this, they had for some time been exempt from the requirement of sacrificing. This was now to change dramatically.

Pagan priests solemnly sacrificing before Diocletian and Galerius encountered difficulties in divining the omens in the entrails of the sacrificial victims, and Christian attendants of the emperor standing close by had made the sign of the cross; as Lactantius says: '... they put the immortal sign on their foreheads. At this the demons were chased away and the holy rites interrupted.'[18] The soothsayers were clearly disturbed and angered, blaming the presence of the Christians. Diocletian 'in furious passion' reacted instantly and ordered all present to sacrifice or be scourged. Commanding officers in the army were notified that all soldiers should be enjoined to follow suit on pain of being deprived of their rank and discharged from service, which subsequently a great many were. Over the next few years the persecution intensified, turning increasingly to acts of violence against persons and property. The imperial edicts were enforced unequally across the empire with Galerius, whose Dacian mother was a votary of the mountain gods, at the spearhead of the campaign, and Diocletian still showing some inclination to resist acts of bloodshed. In the west, in Gaul and Britain, Constantius Chlorus, anxious to preserve the Tetrarchy, declined to persecute Christians themselves but felt obliged to order the destruction of church property. Consequently the western half of the empire suffered rather less and may in any case have proved more accommodating in its attitudes towards the edicts. The effects in the east, on the other hand, were catastrophic as Galerius embarked on an orgy of bloodletting which got worse once Diocletian was out of the way.

Although Diocletian had never intended that the suppression of the Church should result in unwarranted violence against the persons of Christians, it would have been unusually naïve of him to believe that it was not a probable outcome of his policy, particularly when its implementation was in the hands of someone like Galerius. Diocletian was, as we have seen, deeply pagan by inclination himself and may have been waiting for a pretext to reduce the Church's influence by removing its legal status, granted by Gallienus, as a permitted organisation. After what Lactantius describes as continual pressure from Galerius, in 304 Diocletian abandoned his public role and the following year abdicated, retiring to his palace in Split on his native Dalmatian coast.[19] But his final act before withdrawing was to issue an edict that all Roman citizens must offer sacrifice or face the death penalty. This was the ultimate sanction. Many Christians went to their deaths rather than give up their most sacred principle, church buildings were pulled down, including one in full sight of the imperial palace at Nicomedia, and holy objects and furnishings were looted. We do not know from the evidence available whether the destruction of church property also involved the appropriation of church funds, but it is inconceivable that the actions against Christians, their clergy, their worship and whole way of life did not include seizing the precious resources of the treasure chest, set aside as it was to finance all aspects of Christian activity including support for those in need.

Galerius, now Diocletian's successor in the east, continued the policy with even greater fervour and encountered an intransigence which resulted in many new martyrs being added to the Church. However, some years later on his deathbed he seems to have shown some grudging remorse for his actions, restoring the Church's rights on condition 'that they offend not against good order' and that they pray to God for his welfare and that of the public. The persecution was over but much harm had been done, which left deep-seated and lasting scars particularly regarding the future unity of Christendom.

Although the Great Persecution was widespread across the empire, paradoxically its long-term effects proved more damaging in those areas where Christians had actually suffered less and over a shorter period of time, as was generally the case in the west, quite apart from the more lenient attitudes of the western rulers. Here there had tended to be a polarisation of views, with some Christian communities trying to accede to the state's demands without compromising themselves – a largely untenable position after all – whilst others were blind to any accommodation with the authorities. The seeds of schism had been sown and the ground was to produce a rich harvest of bitterness and division, leaving the whole Church, east and west, wide open to extremists like the heretical presbyter Arius and the fanatically orthodox bishop, Epiphanius of Salamis. But these were fresh storms, as yet a generation away. Recovering from the devastating effects of persecution was destined to take the Church well into the fourth century. Its whole infrastructure had been severely damaged and, in some instances, totally demolished. Besides the normal ongoing need to support the poor, a new category of dependants had been created. Many Christian families had lost their breadwinner either by martyrdom or imprisonment, and others who managed to escape the ultimate penalty had lost their jobs and the means of survival. It must be considered one of the extraordinary facts of early Christian history that the Church succeeded in recouping its losses and recovering its poise as well and as quickly as it did.

Even in the darkest days for the Church under Diocletian and Galerius, the mood of the public generally was changing in favour of greater tolerance. People had lost the appetite for bloody reprisals and for the wholesale destruction of property directed at pious and harmless individuals amongst whom they counted friends, neighbours and even members of their own families. Christianity had become conspicuous, albeit as a minority faith, and Christians' devotion to each other and the needs of the poor, even in the face of violent repression, was exemplary and in sharp contrast to the *modus vivendi* of pagan society. More than a century before the Great Persecution commentators like Aristides of Athens and Tertullian had remarked on Christians' devotion, but these commendations in no way lessened the determination of the Fathers to ensure that the strictest standards of behaviour continued to be maintained whatever the circumstances. Cyprian in his *Treatise I, On the unity of the Church* admonishes the faithful that there has been a deterioration in the commitment to providing for the poor.

> But in us unanimity is diminished in proportion as liberality of working is decayed. Then they used to give up for sale houses and estates; and that they might lay up for themselves treasures in heaven, presented to the apostles the price of them, to be distributed for the use of the poor. But now we do not even give the tenths from our patrimony; and while our Lord bids us sell, we rather buy and increase our store. Thus has the vigour of faith dwindled away from us; thus has the strength of believers grown weak.

These were harsh words indeed, but despite their severity the bishop ends with a rallying cry intended to exhort and encourage his readers to better things.

> Let us, beloved brethren, arouse ourselves as much as we can ... Let our light shine in good works, and glow in such wise as to lead us from the night of this world to the daylight of eternal brightness.

This was the kind of message that was calculated to inspire the Church to greater deeds of sacrifice, especially in times of hardship, which in turn resonated with pagan society and recalled the golden age of Rome when a man's heroic acts accorded him a special place amongst his peers. As much as anything could, it advanced the process of Christianisation by linking the moral life of Christians with all that was best in the pagan heritage. If the ancient gods were indeed falling silent, it was because the Christian God was now speaking in their stead and in language pagans could understand. Even the pagan emperor Julian, seventy years hence in the middle of the fourth century, was moved to comment grudgingly on the outstanding quality of the Christian way of life: '... And the impious Galileans (i.e. Christians) support not merely their own poor, but ours as well'.

Furthermore, Christian morality and the moral direction which the Church provided both set it apart and at the same time furnished an example of rectitude in the conduct of personal life. Moral rigour was imposed on all aspects of an individual's life, and the community assumed a corporate responsibility, exercised hierarchically through the bishop as leader, for ensuring that the necessary checks and balances were in place to regulate behaviour according to the Church's strict code of ethics. The message this conveyed was not lost on pagan society. A number of secular writers noted with approval the austerity of a Christian lifestyle, particularly with regard to sexual morals, and the determination with which this was observed in the face of all kinds of human temptation was genuinely admired. The doctor Galen (*c.* 129–99) whilst critical of Christianity's non-scientific basis, nevertheless commented approvingly on the steadfastness of Christians, their sexual restraint, moderation in eating and drinking and sense of justice. He observed:

> Their contempt of death is patent to us every day, and likewise their restraint in cohabitation. For they include not only men but also women who refrain from cohabiting all their lives; and they also number individuals who in self-discipline and self-control, have attained a pitch not inferior to that of genuine philosophers.

A little earlier in the second century and thus a near contemporary of Galen was the Greek doctor Soranus from Ephesus, who in a surviving medical treatise ascribed to him, extolled the practice of continuous virginity which he thought carried with it certain health benefits. Although he was not specifically citing the experience of the Christian way of life, since the topic of chastity in marriage was already a matter of interest to pagan philosophers, it is clear that he admired all those who emulated this ideal. Admiration for the qualities which enabled Christians to practise such restraint is also reflected in the Discourses of the Stoic philosopher, Epictetus, as recorded by the pagan writer Arrian in the first half of the second century. He remarks that some individuals become fearless through madness, but 'the Galileans through habit'; a compliment, if a somewhat oblique one, on the consistency of Christian self-discipline.

It has been said that, lacking the ritual boundaries of Judaism, Christians made sexuality carry the burden of the difference between themselves and pagans. Most prominent Christian writers of the period certainly have something to say in praise of strict sexual behaviour and of the special virtue acquired by those who trod the path of denial. Celibacy in fact was more and more felt to be the appropriate status for those who assumed positions of leadership in the Christian communities. However, in the writings of the Fathers there is much ambivalence on the subject of celibacy. Tertullian in chapter 3 of a treatise written to his wife rather defensively upholds his view that marriage in itself is good, but celibacy preferable. He then devotes the whole of another treatise (number 5) to an exhortation on the virtues of chastity, both before and during marriage as well as following the death of a spouse. At about the same period we find Athenagoras the Athenian, described as a philosopher and Christian, speaking of marriage as simply and solely a means to the procreation of children:

> Therefore ... we despise the things of this life ... each of us reckoning her his wife whom he has married according to the laws laid down by us, and that only for the purpose of having children.

Clement of Alexandria, on the other hand took a very different stance on sexual activity, rejecting the view being propounded by Gnostics that it was incompatible with the higher values. By the mid-fourth century the Council of

Gangra (*c*. 340) condemned the rigorists who opposed marriage, although soon after Pope Damasus decreed celibacy for all the clergy. He was in all probability confirming a practice already well established in the western half of the empire and one which was less strictly observed in the east.

Reassembling the bricks and mortar of classical society into a Christian edifice was much more than a matter of advocating exemplary personal behaviour, however. Although public attitudes had started to reflect the changing circumstances of the times and were reinforced by the more tolerant emperors, the forces of reaction were still powerful enough to fight for their old-world values and Christianity did not maintain its toehold in society without a struggle. Pagan leaders and intellectuals may have been promoting a dying cause, but the transformation of Roman society was destined to be a lengthy if ineluctable process. Even by the time of Constantine's death the majority of the inhabitants of the empire were still pagan. Whereas it was to be expected that conservative élites would seek to preserve their traditional lifestyle, the curious fact of the third century – and one not easily explained – is the extent to which the ordinary citizen adapted to social change. In many ways it was the man in the street who was ahead of the game, and for him Christianity appeared to be offering something that was missing from the life of the Graeco-Roman cities.[20] As a salvation religion it provided a sense of direction and purpose that enabled Christians to carry on through the vicissitudes of the age with the promise of deliverance in the hereafter guaranteed, by the rite of baptism, for those who were henceforth the Lord's Elect. Significantly, those aspects of the life of Jesus that most appealed to third-century men and women were not those that spoke of his human sufferings – his humanity was not emphasised – but those that declared his divine power over demons and his conquest of death. The imagery of Christ the Conqueror, *Christus Victor*, runs through all the mainstream teaching of the Church, from Irenaeus of Lyons in the second century to John of Damascus in the eighth. The human face that Christianity held up to the world consequently compensated for this emphasis on soteriology by stressing the importance of social concern. Whilst urban life had hitherto revolved around the social and religious conventions of classical antiquity, a caring Christian-based society was evolving that bore testimony to the very different, less secure, less assured, Mediterranean world. Through its own acts of supreme confidence in taking social risks the Church was to succeed at precisely those points where paganism was losing its grip.

The continuing development of Christian social services not only enhanced the Church's reputation as a socially-concerned organisation, it also gave the well-off in the community the opportunity to demonstrate solidarity with the poor and hence to acquire a new élitist role as 'friends of the poor', thus underlining in a socially acceptable way the inequalities in society. Again a snapshot of the Christian community in Rome in the third century serves to illustrate how far the Church had come since the days of Marcus Aurelius and Commodus. As the focus of empire, Rome was naturally the centre of the Roman world, the seat of government and the Senate, the hub of social and commercial activity and the place where religious tradition was most particularly enshrined in its temples and priesthoods. Thus it was to Rome that some of the first generation of Christian leaders, such as the Apostles Peter and Paul, had gravitated and to which Christians had continued to resort from all corners of the empire. The community, therefore, was not only of ancient foundation but had expanded steadily over the years and had attracted converts from all sections of society – including, as we have seen, the Imperial Household. Because of its position, the city of Rome and its environs supported a large population of which, it is estimated, as many as 100,000 people were in regular receipt of free distributions of corn during the long years of economic decline in Italy and throughout the empire. The size of the Christian community placed a corresponding burden in relative terms upon the Church, the number of whose dependants had similarly increased. Cornelius, who became Bishop of Rome in 251, at the time of the Decian persecution and following the martyrdom of his predecessor, Pope Fabianus, wrote to Fabius, Bishop of Antioch, on the subject of the Novatian schism and included an account of the financial and social responsibilities he had inherited. (The letter is quoted at length by Eusebius in his *Ecclesiastical History*, Bk 6, ch. 43). In 248, we are told, the church in Rome had no fewer than 155 clergy to maintain together with readers and janitors, and provided financial support to 1,500 widows and other needy persons. Whilst the sheer weight of numbers renders the Roman situation somewhat atypical, there is no reason to suppose that similar conditions did not obtain in other Christian centres, although few can have enjoyed the extensive resources available to Christians in Rome or in a city such as Carthage. It was, for example, these churches which were able to donate large capital sums to Christian brethren in Africa and Cappadocia for the ransoming of captives seized in barbarian raids in 254 and 256. The gravity of the situation is captured for us by Cyprian in his *Epistle 59* when he responds to the Numidian bishops deploring their news that so many of 'our brothers and sisters' were being held prisoner. Immediate aid is promised for the ransoming of the captives. 'Our brotherhood' he writes, 'considering all these things according to your letter, and sorrowfully examining, have all promptly and willingly and liberally gathered together supplies for the brethren ... we have then sent you a sum of 100,000 sesterces, which have been collected here in the church over which by the Lord's mercy we preside, by the contributions of the clergy and people established with us, which you will there dispense with what diligence you may.' 100,000 sesterces was an immense sum of money for the times. In times of public emergency nearer home the clergy played a major role in organising food supplies and even ensuring that the dead were buried properly and decently. By the middle of the third century the Church was leading the Mediterranean world as the principal investor in people.

However, despite having often significant means at their disposal, the clergy did not distribute help in an indiscriminate fashion; the constantly high level of demand for charitable relief coming from so many quarters required to be governed by strict criteria. Although the Church had a reputation for extending a helping hand to non-members, it was dependants of the Christian community itself who became the chief recipients of its accumulated offerings. These were deposited with the bishop and came to be regarded as part of the offertory within the liturgical context of the celebration of the Eucharist, although not necessarily being presented on that occasion. Since the development of an ecclesiastical hierarchy, within which the functions of office holders had become more clearly defined, bishops had borne the prime responsibility for managing the resources of the Church. In its earliest days the Christian community's collections of alms were kept in less than secure conditions in the communal treasure chest. But as the Church grew and became a property-owning organisation, with all that that implies in the building and maintenance of places of worship, now replacing private houses, with salaried staff and charitable commitments, its business life demanded rather more sophisticated treatment. The days of gifts in kind were largely a thing of the past.

During the reign of Commodus (180–192), as has been mentioned in chapter 5 above, a bank had been established with the assistance of Carpophorus, a Christian with a position in the emperor's household. Wealthy members of the Church lodged money with him which was then placed in a bank in the Piscina Publica, the public fish market, one of the fourteen quarters of Rome, where money dealing took place. Over a period of time the deposits were said to amount to a considerable sum. Very quickly these arrangements actually ran into serious trouble at the hands of a dishonest servant of Carpophorus, called Callistus, who embezzled the money and attempted to abscond by ship. On being apprehended he was returned to Rome, confined, released, caused a disturbance in a Jewish synagogue and ultimately was deported to the Sardinian mines. Even this did not by any means mark the end of the Callistus story. Eventually released at the behest of Commodus's Christian concubine, Marcia, Callistus inveigled himself into holy orders and, to the disgust of many, especially the writer and bishop Hippolytus, crowned his notorious career by becoming Bishop of Rome and therefore, one supposes, Pope.[21] The Callistus incident, although the action of a wayward youth, presumably damaged the Church's credibility for a time, especially as he had been treated with no small degree of leniency; his subsequent behaviour after ordination left more lasting scars upon the Church's reputation and altogether illustrates some of the difficulties encountered by the Church in the laborious process of becoming a recognised institution within Roman society. However, the initially abortive banking arrangements survived these problems and were re-established and strengthened during the reign of Septimius Severus.

Our main source for the Callistus story is Hippolytus who devotes almost three chapters of his work *The Refutation of All Heresies* to a highly personalised and vituperous account of the former slave's nefarious life and dubious theology. Hippolytus was the disciple of the Apostolic Father, Irenaeus of Lyons, himself a pupil of the great Polycarp of Smyrna, who was said, in turn, to have been a disciple of St John, and therefore stood in a distinguished line of apostolic orthodoxy. Irenaeus' principal theological work is a treatise against the Gnostics, which he was moved to write after a visit to Rome where he encountered the Montanist and Valentinian heresies in the senior leadership of the church. In a situation similar to his former master, Hippolytus confronted two consecutive bishops of Rome, Zephyrinus and Callistus, for what he claimed were their errors in doctrine and viciousness of life. It must be remembered, that coming from such an orthodox tradition Hippolytus was inevitably a rigorist in matters of church discipline and doctrine. The question we have to answer is whether he is being unfair and mistaken, to put it no higher than that, in his savage condemnation of Callistus. Clearly he had little tolerance for Callistus' rather liberal opinions, for example, on the acceptability of marriages between upper-class women and men of lower social status, unions which were, in any case, expressly forbidden under Roman law. Furthermore the Callistan view that the Church, after the analogy of Noah's ark, which contained both clean and unclean beasts, should properly grant forgiveness to those who had sinned after receiving baptism, must surely be a reflection of his own personal history. Even if we accept only the broad outlines of Callistus' early career, his relaxed attitudes on questions of morality, as bishop of Rome, are enough to lend confirmation to the fact that he would have been extremely uncomfortable with rigorist views on past behaviour which condemned him outright and called into question the validity of his orders as priest and bishop. On matters of doctrinal orthodoxy, Callistus treads on equally shifting sands. At that time the church in Rome was being vexed by the heretical opinions of one Sabellius, a little-known figure in the third century, who advanced the view that the Father and the Son are one and the same being, considered in two different aspects. Although the precise details of the heresy need not detain us here, Hippolytus stood at the opposite extreme to Sabellius and was scathing about Callistus who tried, unsuccessfully, to reach a compromise position. When the latter became bishop of Rome he excommunicated Sabellius, an act that totally failed to impress Hippolytus. What conclusions can therefore be reached on the question of the character of Callistus? There is sufficient evidence from his subsequent behaviour as bishop of Rome to support the general outline of his early life as propounded by the, admittedly, ultra-orthodox and prejudiced Hippolytus, and although almost all we known of Callistus' later career comes from the same critical hand, there is no reason to suppose that his critic deliberately manufactured evidence against him for no good reason. With the backing of his supporters, Hippolytus put himself up as bishop of Rome in opposition to Callistus; an act that might be considered highly irregular, and thus call into question his own moral standing, were it not for the fact that he clearly believed that Callistus had no legitimacy in the first place. Someone who was such a rigorist in matters of church discipline and doctrine, would otherwise never have contemplated a course of action which would brand him as a schismatic. Hippolytus would have been appalled at the later description of himself as the first anti-pope of history. In the event the Church sat on the fence and canonised both men!

Those changes in imperial policy towards Christians in the third century which resulted in oppression, coupled with the effects of economic decline, together produced a range of social conditions which resulted in increasing numbers of human casualties presenting themselves at the doors of churches in search of succour, as well as those who suffered incarceration for their faith in local and foreign prisons. Large-scale deprivation takes more than a change in political administration to be cured and the Church's resources were to be stretched to the limit well into the reign of Constantine. Although new freedoms were to be conferred through imperial rescript, a golden age for the Church in terms of having resolved its many domestic problems was not, in fact, just around the corner.

Constantine may have been about to unlock the door of opportunity but the Church was soon to discover that there were some individuals, only too eager to accept the invitation, against whom the door was better kept firmly barred.

Notes

1. See Peter Brown, *The World of Late Antiquity* and *The Making of Late Antiquity*.
2. See Michael Grant, *The Climax of Rome*.
3. For a good introduction to military affairs under the Empire, see Graham Webster, *The Roman Imperial Army*.
4. For further discussion on the size of the Roman army, see Averil Cameron, *The Later Roman Empire* III, The New Empire: Diocletian, p. 30 seq. London, Duckworth, 1978.
5. For further reading, see G. W. Bowerstock, *Julian the Apostate*, London, Duckworth, 1978 and for an in-depth look at his intellectual development, see Polymnia Athenassiadi, *Julian, An Intellectual Biography*, paperback edition, London and New York, Routledge, 1992.
6. See Robert Grant, *Gods and the One God*.
7. See Marta Sordi, *Christians and the Roman Empire*, chapter 2.
8. See Eusebius, *Ecclesiastical History*, bk. 6, 1, Nicene and Post Nicene Fathers, vol. 1. Also Marta Sordi, above, chapter 5.
9. See Eusebius above, Bk. 6, chapter 28.
10. *Ibid.*, chapter 6, p. 39. See also Marta Sordi above, chapter 6.
11. Eusebius above, chapter 7 and Marta Sordi above, chapter 7.
12. Eusebius above, chapter 8.
13. Averil Cameron points out in her chapter on 'Late Roman Social Structures and the Late Roman Economy' in *The Mediterranean World in Late Antiquity* that there has been a re-evaluation in recent years of theories of Rome's decline and fall based, in part, on the

evidence for economic collapse. The literary sources, Cameron says, cannot be taken at face value, e.g. Lactantius, who was heavily biased against Diocletian. According to this view the increase in the size of the army may well be exaggerated. See note 4 of this chapter above.
14. See *ibid.* for Cameron's view that it is by no means certain that Diocletian greatly increased taxation, as is the more traditional view, as opposed to pursuing a revisionist policy with the aim of improving its collection.
15. Lactantius, 'Of the manner in which the persecutors died', chapter 11 in Ante Nicene Fathers, vol. 7, p. 305 seq.
16. *Ibid.*, chapter 14.
17. The philosopher Plotinus was born *c.* 205 probably at Lycopolis in Egypt and died in 270. Along with other late pagan Platonists he was a vehement opponent of Gnosticism and wrote a violent tract against it, attacking its pretentious mythological teachings. (*Enneads*, 11, 9). Plotinus was certainly aware of Christianity although it was his biographer, Porphyry, who became such an implacable opponent of it.
18. Lactantius above, chapter 10.
19. *Ibid.*, chapters 18 and 19.
20. See Peter Brown, *The World of Late Antiquity*.
21. See Hippolytus, 'The Refutation of all Heresies', chapter 7 in Ante Nicene Fathers, vol. 5.

Chapter Seven

Constantine and the Christian Empire

Throughout its three-hundred-year history the succession to the leadership of the Roman Empire had often been a hit-and-miss affair with some notable 'misses' featuring amongst the long list of appointees. All too frequently it became a matter of commanding the support of the Praetorian Guard, not always the best judges of suitability for the highest public office, or appealing to the loyalty of those legions of the army which were prepared to impose their will, by force if necessary, and to place the diadem on the head of their chosen candidate. Constantine's elevation was no less opportunistic. He had joined his father, the Emperor Constantius I Chlorus, who was campaigning in Britain against the Picts in Caledonia when he died of natural causes on 25 July 306 at York. True to form, the local garrison proclaimed Constantine as Augustus in his father's stead.[1] The story of his subsequent rise to the sole mastery of the Roman world is well known.[2] His career as emperor spanned thirty-one crowded years and he left the pagan empire of Rome Christian in name if not wholly in practice.

There seems little doubt that Constantine's vision in the sky of the Cross of Christ on the eve of the Battle of the Milvian Bridge and his diplomatic adoption of the *Chi Rho* monogram, as recorded severally by his biographers, was part of an excellent and well thought-out strategy to embrace the protection of the Christian God.[3] He was above all a pragmatist whose overriding concerns were political unity and social stability. But he also cherished ambitions of universalism. Constantine aspired to the greatest vision of all, to unite the world (and by that he meant more than just the world of Rome and its empire) under One God, One Empire and One Emperor.

The first of these three aims was already in the wind, since a drift towards monotheism had long been occupying the minds of philosophical thinkers even from as far back as the time of Plato, and had received added impetus during the course of the third century. So although born a pagan and indeed remaining one for almost the whole of his life, an adherent to Sol Invictus, the cult of his Balkan ancestors, Constantine already subscribed to an essentially monotheistic belief, and the reunification of the empire under one emperor, to his way of thinking, was contingent on the acceptance of one supreme deity. For its part Christianity was continuing to consolidate its position in Roman society and was thus helping to create conditions under which he would be able to recognise a religious and cultural reality at the heart of his political vision. In order to accomplish all his aims Constantine required no sudden and bloody revolution, although the systematic elimination of certain of his co-Augusti, together with the execution of his first wife and son, show a willingness, not exceptional for the age, to use the means of violence to achieve his ends. The task he set himself and from which he refused to be diverted was only partially to be realised but even so was magnificent both in its scope and its implications for the Church and the empire.

A universal vision, if it is to stand any chance of coming to fruition, demands a universalist policy. Moreover it has to be a policy that attracts the support and respect of diverse peoples who constitute a multicultural state, and that therefore is linked to a cultural institution with the potential for universal appeal. Such an institution was Christianity, very much still a minority within the empire but a deeply influential one, many of whose members held key positions in government and civic life. In thus according Christianity official status Constantine was acknowledging not only that it was becoming an integral part of national life but also that it contained all the essential ingredients to form the core of his universalist policy. Nor was it a thousand miles away from his own religious background, and making the transition was to prove less demanding in intellectual terms than might be imagined. In his personal life the change occurred rather by degrees as he began to recognise and establish his own status as a 'friend of God', but not being one to discard his heritage lightly, his very late baptism and formal reception into the Church is perhaps understandable. It also has to be borne in mind that Constantine's deferment of baptism was not necessarily an unusual step for a newly 'converted' Christian to take at this time, if indeed it is even valid to use this word to describe the emperor's desire to embrace the Christian faith. Some Christians opted to remain catechumens for the greater part of their lives, accepting the rite of baptism only in old age or, in many cases, as an act of death-bed repentance. Taking a well-nigh irrevocable step such as this had considerable ramifications for personal life; sexual morals apart, the Church's rules on matters like divorce, attending the theatre or the baths, to name but a few, were strict to the point of being oppressive. Avoiding mortal sin, therefore, during a normal person's lifetime was no easy task and many chose to wait as long as they reasonably could before taking the plunge. Inevitably some of the bishops, like Basil of Caesarea, Gregory of Nazianzus and Augustine, were less than enthusiastic about this practice.

The Christianisation of the empire was similarly a gradual process, in the course of which the Edict of Milan, which effectively confirmed and extended the earlier Edict of Toleration of Galerius by further strengthening the Church's legal position in Roman society, was a crucial step along the way. It was issued in 313 by both Constantine and his co-Augustus Licinius who at this stage was still master of the east, having eliminated Maximinus II Daia, and was destined to remain so for another nine years until he was finally defeated by Constantine at the Battle of Chrysopolis in 324. More like notes of guidance for provincial governors than an imperial edict as such, the Milan statement was followed by a series of measures granting additional privileges to Christian communities.[4]

Christian clergy and their congregations must have been overwhelmed by the emperor's beneficence, as official support on this kind of scale was previously unknown. Church property was removed from liability to taxation, and provincial government was mandated to supply building materials for the construction of new churches as well as meeting the costs of labour. Church officials received financial support in the pursuit of their duties and even allocations of food and clothing were made available to those who required assistance. Constantine had inaugurated, in c. 326, his new imperial capital of Constantinople on the site of the ancient city of Byzantium, close to the scene of his victory over Licinius. In 332 he introduced the dole to the city in the form of bread rather than grain and it is said that some 80,000 citizens benefited from it. At times of famine during his reign Constantine gave the Church the prime responsibility for administering the grain supplies in the larger cities to those in hardship. Wherever charitable relief is mentioned, the same disadvantaged groups as in previous generations were the recipients – namely, widows, orphans and the very poor, although this time clerics sometimes appear on the lists for the first time. Some churches received generous allocations, no doubt if there were large-scale local problems: a Byzantine writer, for example, states that the church in Antioch had enough grain at its disposal to meet the needs of about a thousand people for a whole year, not inconsiderable resources even for one of the larger Christian communities. Financial assistance for the clergy may well have been paid in the form of emoluments for their role in administering the dole to the faithful needy; clearly there was an expectation that only the orthodox would so benefit and that Arians, for example, and other schismatics would be excluded. Two Christian historians of the period, Eusebius and Theodoret, tend to place their own particular emphasis on the categories of needy individuals requiring support, depending on the kind of picture each wishes to portray of how Constantine directed his ecclesiastical policy. Most commentators, however, agree that his policy was based on a need for national unity and on proof of the efficacy of the Christian God in affording the emperor protection and enabling him to triumph over his enemies. Constantine's part as a 'friend of God' was to bestow his munificence upon the Church in endowments, grants, favours, magnificent buildings and charitable donations. A man not without a marked degree of personal vanity and a very clear vision of his role, he came to see himself almost *in loco Christi*: during his lifetime he virtually governed the Church, appointing all bishops and by his presence exercising influence over its Councils, and in death had his tomb surrounded by sarcophagi of the twelve Apostles, a final symbolic act the significance of which was not intended to be lost on his contemporaries or on his imperial successors.

But his policy was destined to fall short of his ambition. Roman society was too conservative to change overnight and the Church was manifestly not up to it. A national religion, which is what Constantine hoped to bring about, cannot be created by imperial rescript. It must win the hearts and minds of all sections of the population, and that takes time, patience and at least a show of unity. The Church was becoming hopelessly divided within itself and serious doctrinal divisions in a minority religion do little to commend it to a sceptical pagan majority who, at the very least, have longevity on their side. Two major religious dissensions wreaked havoc within the Constantinian church, neither of which was destined to be resolved during the emperor's lifetime. The Donatist controversy originated in Carthage in North Africa and was one of the bitter legacies of the Diocletian persecution. Some clergy wishing to escape reprisals had agreed to hand over the Holy Scriptures to officials charged with the responsibility, amongst other things, of collecting and destroying church property. Others made a show of cooperating by trying to pass over heretical or secular works instead, even in one instance medical treatises. Both groups were regarded as *lapsi*, that is, lapsed Christians who had compromised their faith by these actions. The Donatists who followed the strict line taken by Donatus, Bishop of Carthage, in this matter, refused to accept any who had so stained the Church and shamed those who had suffered martyrdom. On the other side of the argument were those who felt that to decline to co-operate was merely to court disaster and put the whole Church at risk; hence they were disposed towards leniency for church leaders who had given in to the state's demands. Constantine, despite referring the issue to a meeting of bishops in Rome and then to a review by the Council of Arles in 314 failed to resolve the dispute, which developed into a full-blown schism that lasted a hundred years.

An even greater threat to the unity of Christendom was posed by the controversy arising from the beliefs of a presbyter of Alexandria named Arius, who held that God the Son must be inferior to God the Father, the First Cause of creation. Arius was immensely popular, especially in his native city, and he attracted a considerable following of young women and of dock workers for whom, apparently, he composed religious shanties. Many distinguished churchmen of the day were swayed by Arius' views, including the church historian Eusebius, but the Council of Nicea in 325 came down against the Arians, and Eusebius hastily recanted rather than face exile and disgrace. His account of the Council's proceedings is a somewhat ill-disguised attempt to play down the problem in order to enhance his own rehabilitation. But Arianism was not to be so easily suppressed and in one form or another it continued to divide the Church for centuries, finding supporters amongst Constantine's own family and becoming a feature of the church in the Balkans.

Constantine's social welfare policy, the implementation of which was largely in the hands of episcopal administrators, ran into difficulties on account of the sheer scale of the task. The preferential treatment of orthodox Christians in the distribution of the grain dole only served to fuel resentment and, indeed, one of Constantine's successors, Julian, who in any case favoured a national return to paganism, removed the administration of it from the Church and placed it in the hands of pagan priests, a policy yet again reversed by his successor, Jovian.

The grain dole in the cities went some way to relieving real hardship, but it excluded some sections of the urban population and did little to alleviate the plight of the rural poor. The Church's charitable work needed to be heavily supplemented by the continuation of private donations. The new Constantinian basilicas became focal points not only for the collection of alms but also for the congregation of the poor and needy, who crowded around its entrance and even slept in its precincts, awaiting the charity of their better-off fellow citizens. To respond to their pleas was seen by the Church as an efficacious way of making reparation for the small everyday venial sins that beset the faithful. (More serious wrongdoing was dealt with through acts of public penance performed in the presence of the bishop.) In this way, the poor in need of the support of the Christian community became a metaphor for the sinner in need of the mercy and redemption of God. Socially and financially-secure church members, together with the bishops and other church leaders who began to take the place of the civic notables of the age of the Antonines and the Severans, accordingly viewed the poor in an altogether different light. No longer a merely disregarded sub-class on the fringes of society, they became the means by which the churchgoer might enter into a new relationship with God, and hence they acquired a certain status as the instruments of God's grace. In the fourth-century Constantinian church their role was a complete departure from that of *clientela* under the old patronage system of the Graeco-Roman cities. After all, the poor were powerless and, unlike *clientela*, had nothing to offer in return for the charitable gifts they received: in this context reciprocity was meaningless. This appealed to the new Christian élite precisely because it was a one-way street, with none of the tensions inherent in *quid pro quo* relationships.

Since the days of the Jesus movement and the Pauline mission women had always played a significant part in the Church's life, an important factor which is only now receiving the attention it deserves from modern scholars.[5] In some communities they were the linchpin upon which the survival of the sect depended, by providing suitable accommodation or attending to the needs of the sick and helpless and, in the case of wealthy upper-class women, putting their own considerable financial resources at the disposal of the Church's treasure chest. Their role became increasingly prominent as church leaders extolled the virtues of sexual abstinence exemplified by virgins and widows and frequently enjoined on all Christians. In the eyes of the clergy, the lavish contributions made by women of substance and the influence they exercised as a consequence was a potential source of embarrassment. Now the poor afforded an excellent opportunity to channel these funds in ways that were completely in harmony with Christ's own commandment about love towards one's neighbour. And the emperor's mother, Helena, took the lead in demonstrations of generosity to the Church which became almost as legendary as her son's. Her lavish building plans and relentless shopping expeditions for relics of Christ and the saints encouraged Christian women generally to contribute time and resources to supporting the missionary and caring work of the church. Helena made active involvement in church work fashionable.

Whilst the Church had been developing into a property-owning organisation, a process to which Constantine's ecclesiastical policy gave added impetus, there were many pastors as well as rank-and-file members, especially those struggling in depressed rural areas, who felt uncomfortable with the image of the Church as a landed proprietor. To such Christians this was a betrayal of the ancient ideals of the Jesus movement when everything was held in common for the benefit of all, and which they believed could still be valid even in the boom days of the fourth century. But they were swimming against the tide. The character of the Church was changing and a return to a more ascetic manner of life would be achieved only by withdrawing from the freneticism of the town and the city to the solitariness of the desert. Since Constantine had removed Augustan penalties for celibacy, Christian asceticism became more attractive from the legal aspect of inheritance. This new asceticism, pioneered by men like Pachomius and Antony, demanded separation from the world rather than seeking to change it from within, and although many of the desert fathers gradually assumed not only exemplary but consultative and didactic roles, the movement was essentially one based on personal communion with God away from the hurly-burly of everyday affairs. Many varieties of the ascetic life, by no means confined to a desert existence, developed, including a number of like-minded upper-class ladies who associated together in what were more or less aristocratic households. Nevertheless, by its very nature asceticism, at least in theory, rested on the foundation of poverty, to which was added the strictures of chastity and obedience and its appeal was surprisingly attractive to some Christians who wished perhaps to recover a quality of living in the presence of God that the Church seemed to have lost. Yet, despite their seclusion, the leading holy men and women of the desert were to remain remarkably close to the core of the Church's involvement in religious and secular affairs and, by the end of the fourth century, must have numbered many thousands of practitioners.

However, the ascetic movement posed two major problems. In terms of a national policy of integration between Church and state it was divisive, since it represented a parallel style of living outside normal community existence and beyond the immediate control of the church authorities, and hence of the Church by the state – or, more accurately, by the emperor. Among the many dispensations granted to the Christian clergy by Constantine, their exemption from civic duties had been intended to release them for the better performance of their religious duties. Repudiation of these responsibilities by resorting to the eremitic life was not at all part of his plan for the Church. Whilst the growth of heretical tendencies remained the most serious and intractable problem for the successful implementation of Constantine's policy, the ascetic's ethos of autonomy, nominally within but in reality outside the jurisdiction of the Church, only compounded the difficulties. Furthermore, from the Church's point of view it placed an additional burden on its overstretched resources: although many ascetics lived in conditions that could be described as absolute poverty, their continued survival depended on at least minimal subsistence, and Christians who much admired their example but had no wish to emulate it were eager to offer support in the form of meeting basic needs. Of course, some hermits did maintain themselves by cultivating a small patch of ground close to their cell, and those who opted for the coenobitic life strove as far as possible to be self-sufficient. But there were many solitaries whose habit it was to confine themselves for

Constantine and the Christian Empire   109

long periods of time in walled-up cells or who otherwise restricted their own movements, and who therefore became totally dependent upon the ministrations of others. This was bound to have implications for the Church's charitable work amongst the urban and rural populations where there was no diminution of the numbers requiring help, as a whole new constituency of dependants had been created. The Church consequently continued for some time to be hard-pressed financially in trying to meet its increasing commitments. Even the emperor's generosity to the poor in the provision of both food and clothing, extolled, and probably exaggerated, by Eusebius, which was, nevertheless, to become well-nigh legendary, did not lessen the burden to any great extent.

As the Christian community entrenched itself deeper in the fabric of the empire, and the visible evidence of this was all around in magnificent new buildings or sumptuously refurbished and converted pagan temples, so the status of the bishops rose as leaders in society, as protectors of the poor and as guardians of rich, influential women whose wealth could be directed into works of mercy. Churches became the new civic centres around which urban life started to revolve. There, too, the fugitive could seek asylum, the slave could be manumitted and the 'treasure chest' be opened for the relief of the needy. Paganism and Christianity had already fought out their conflict in the heavens, and the Christian God had been declared triumphant. Now the battle became an earth-bound one for the hearts and minds of men and women. This too was to be resolved in Christianity's favour, but chiefly because Christians and non-Christians alike shared a common culture which gave expression to the concept and the reality of being a citizen of the Late Roman state.

Christianisation may have played a lesser role in the process of developing this culture than has popularly been supposed. The symbols by which it was recognised would have been intensely familiar both to pagans, who had scarcely even rubbed shoulders with the Christian Church, and to Christians who had enjoyed the benefits of a traditional classical education. Perhaps the most outstanding example of this development is given by Peter Brown on page 12 of *Authority and the Sacred* (Cambridge University Press, 1995). A well-off Christian, Valentinus, commissioned an artist who had worked for the Pope as well as other influential Christians, to produce a handsome version of the *Calendar of 354*. The finished work used both Christian symbols, as well as symbols taken from the pagan Roman cultus, with which his patron would have been all too familiar, to illustrate the various months. We are instantly reminded of some of the glories of medieval manuscript decoration and the magnificent sculptural oddities in many western churches, which boldly reassert this continuing tradition. Nevertheless in the post-Constantinian world the official public cults of the pagan gods were being slowly squeezed out of the system, although it was to be at least another generation or two before Christians formed anything like a majority in the empire.[6]

Whatever we may think of Constantine as a man or as an emperor – and he had successes and failures in both roles – it is as the founding father of a universal Church that history should judge him. In certain respects, he must have died a disappointed man. The Church which was to be at the very centre of his grand design for a world united under God, Rome and its emperor was unable to deliver on what was expected of it. Riven by doctrinal controversy, it could never present the united front Constantine envisaged; although orthodoxy asserted itself over the Donatists and Arians, both disagreements were to continue to reverberate long after Constantine's reign had come to an end and, in the case of the latter, even well beyond the period of Late Antiquity. Nevertheless, he deserves the credit history, on the whole, has awarded him for giving the opportunity to the Christian Church to establish itself as a national religious institution, regardless of the fact that his successor, the Emperor Julian, tried to put the clock back and, indeed, had a good many people to cheer him on. Ultimately the triumph was Christianity's and therefore Constantine's.

Of the many rulers of the eastern and western halves of the Roman Empire comparatively few left behind as enduring and rich a legacy as Constantine. Amongst his predecessors

Augustus, Hadrian and Marcus Aurelius must surely figure, and even Diocletian for his long-reaching political and economic policies. Over the succeeding two centuries perhaps Theodosius the Great and Justinian tower above the rest; although with all such 'league tables' comparisons do scant justice to the historical record. Constantine's signal contribution was both political and religious, although the latter was destined to be best remembered. His recognition of the Christian Church, quite apart from his own disputed adoption of Christianity, placed the eastern emperors in a special relationship to the Church; not one of control or domination as has sometimes been claimed, but more of influence, which found no parallel in the west under the barbarian kings, emerging there only much later in the successor kingdoms.

After his death the unity he strove so hard to achieve was to last a mere 140 years until 476 when Romulus Augustulus, the last Roman emperor of the west to occupy the imperial throne, was compelled to vacate it in favour of the barbarian general and Master of the Soldiers, Odoacer.[7] This event has misleadingly been referred to as the fall of the Roman Empire. The reality was rather different because the transition to barbarian government which was in any case confined to the west – the east continued as before under the Byzantine emperors – was so gradual a process that it is doubtful whether the inhabitants of the west would have noticed much difference in the way in which they were governed throughout the entire period of barbarian incursion. Odoacer and his successors retained much of the infrastructure of the Roman state, and for themselves were content to be recognised by Constantinople as kings and consuls rather than displaying any ambitions for the imperial purple.[8] Securing their future was more a matter of acceptance by the eastern empire of a *fait accompli*, coupled with one or two good dynastic marriages with daughters of the imperial house.

There was also a new force to be reckoned with in the rise of the power of the medieval papacy, for which the transfer to barbarian government had presented a remarkable opportunity. Monarchical episcopacy was a well-established fact even before Constantine's policy confirmed the authority of the bishops, and the primacy of the See of Rome, although much contested in the east, was certainly strengthened by the political changes in the west. Already firmly settled at the heart of the Christian community in Rome for the best part of four centuries, the papacy, by the time of Gregory the Great (590–604), was on the verge of creating a new dichotomy between Church and state, in which the power of the Church was to emerge as the most potent force of the future. Meanwhile, in the east from its capital at Constantinople, the New Rome, the theocratic Byzantine Empire was signally failing to prevent the seeds of schism from taking root in a doctrinally-divided Christendom. Although under Justinian (527–65) the universalist vision of Constantine was briefly to be resuscitated, to all intents and purposes it was dead, and it was only a matter of time before the Late Antique world over which he had towered like a colossus would follow it to the grave. By that time, the European Middle Ages had arrived.

NOTES

1. Flavius Valerius Constantinus (Constantine the Great), born 27 February 272 and died 22 May 337. For his early life see Michael Grant, *The Emperor Constantine*, chapter 2.
2. See also the above chapter for Grant's assessment of Lactantius's highly coloured account of how Constantine was passed over for the Caesarship by Galerius, then co-Augustus with Constantine's father, Constantius I Chlorus and subsequently 'escaped' from Galerius's court in order to join his father in Britain.
3. Eusebius, *Vita Constantine* 1. 58. See also Lactantius, *op. cit.*, chapter 49.
4. Eusebius, *Eccl. Hist.* 10.5. Lactantius, *op. cit.*, chapter 48.
5. See especially E. Schussler Fiorenza, *In memory of Her: A Feminist Theological reconstruction of Christian origins*, New York: Crossroads, 1983.
6. For further reading on the Christianisation of the Roman Empire see the following: Averil Cameron, *Christianity and the Rhetoric of Empire*, University of California Press, 1991; R. MacMullen, *Christianizing the Roman Empire, AD 100–400*, Philadelphia: Fortress Press, 1975; R. Lane Fox, *Pagans and Christians*, Harmondsworth, Viking Press, 1986.

7. During the course of the fifth century the authority of the western emperors had been in decline through a succession of ineffectual rulers who became pawns in the hands of their generals, many of whom were of barbarian origin.
8. The title 'king' had always been deeply unpopular in Rome since the Romans expelled the old monarchy nearly one thousand years before, in 510 BC, and set up the Roman Republic. When Augustus established the Principate he knew this only too well and opted for tactful modesty over grandeur. Now another five hundred years had passed and Roman memories were still unbelievably long!

Epilogue

The Roots of Community Care

The great famine which devastated the region of Cappadocia in 368 was described by the theologian, Gregory of Nazianzus, as 'the most severe one ever recorded'. His friend and fellow theologian, Bishop Basil of Caesarea, responded to the crisis in terms which have become a highwater mark in the history of social welfare: 'For by his words and advice,' writes Gregory, 'he opened the stores of those who possessed them, and so, according to the Scriptures dealt food to the hungry, and satisfied the poor with bread, and fed them in time of dearth ... He gathered together the victims of the famine ... men and women, infants, old men, every age which was in distress ... he attended to the bodies and souls of those who needed it, combining personal respect with the supply of their necessity, and so giving them a double relief' (*The Panegyric on St Basil*, NPNF 2, vol. 7, p. 407). Basil's response set a standard for all good community care policies to come; namely, that measures of care should be provided by the community on the basis of identified need and in accordance with the rights of the individual to a life of security within society. But there was another side to it as well.

Christian almsgiving to the poor mirrored that of the Jewish synagogue communities who similarly idealised the concept of absolute poverty, though this was not thought of by either Christians or Jews in a purely materialistic sense, but further implied a deprivation of spiritual values. The *ptochoi*, the 'poor', were those who had not even the basic means of subsistence, to sustain either their natural or religious lives. Social welfare in modern times has focused on the twin concepts of absolute and relative poverty, and public policy and legislation in the field of community care has been primarily concerned to address the problem of attitudes, by speaking of the individual's entitlement to the take-up of social welfare benefits, to the right to have needs met, and to be able to exercise the right of choice. These values form an integral part of what it means to be a caring community, where practical help is combined with dignity and respect for the individual. Nowhere is this more clearly illustrated than by the example set by fourth-century St Basil, who may thus be accounted one of history's earliest social reformers. Whilst the Early Christians emphasised exclusiveness in defining their own communities, in charitable giving they practised the principle of inclusiveness and gained much credit from their pagan contemporaries for so doing. The greatest achievement of their Late Roman descendants was to give the concept of community an entirely new meaning.

The famine of 368 had a impact on society for many years to come. Both Gregory and Basil were forced to address the issue of the stockpiling of grain by rich landowners and merchants, who were reluctant to sell except at grossly inflated prices, thereby denying the poorest and hardest hit access to these vital resources. In his sermon delivered on the Eighth Sunday after Pentecost, Basil takes the lead on behalf of the church in dealing with this matter, and emphasises the notion of community responsibility, which he further explores elsewhere in his homilies. No longer does 'community' refer simply, as in the pre-Constantinian church, to the Christian community gathered in one particular location. When the bishop speaks of it, he has in mind the whole civic body acting with corporate responsibility. And when he addresses the question of poverty, it is in absolute rather than relative terms that he speaks, since that was the effect of the Cappadocian famine on the most vulnerable in the community. The city population itself had almost certainly been swelled by a large influx of starving and destitute people from the surrounding rural areas. The bishop's chosen text for this occasion is from Luke 12:16–18,

> The land of a certain rich man brought forth plenty of fruits. And he thought within himself, saying: What shall

> I do, because I have no room where to bestow my fruits? And he said: This will I do: I will pull down my barns and build greater.

Basil is scathing about the attitude of the rich, concerned only with their own future wellbeing, and their obsession with increasing their personal wealth.

> What scheme will you not set in motion for the sake of gold? For you wheat becomes gold, wine grows into gold, wool is woven into gold. All that is bought and sold, every human activity, brings you gold.

The result of this selfishness is a refusal to acknowledge that the plight of the starving is literally a matter of life and death:

> When I have these new barns filled, you say, then I will distribute something to the poor ... What keeps you from giving now? There are no hungry perhaps? Are your barns not full? Is the price not ready? Is the law of God not plain to you? The hungry are dying before your face. The naked are stiff with cold. The man in debt is held by the throat. And you, you put off your alms, till another day.

But Basil does not merely deal with the practical effects of human selfishness upon the victims of famine. Moral failure to respond to the urgent needs of the time bears environmental consequences too. 'Look how the multitude of our sins forced the seasons to be unnatural'. Here a fourth-century pastor sounds a cautionary note which has a peculiarly prophetic ring for twenty-first-century men and women.

Throughout the whole period of Christian origins, the establishment and maintenance of new communities was a primary concern, and amongst the various strands of New Testament writing different kinds of community can be detected. For example, Matthew's Gospel seems to reflect a community trying to adjust to new circumstances following the destruction of the Temple in 70, and the removal, therefore, of the traditional focal point of Jewish (and, more recently, Jewish-Christian) worship. The Pastoral Epistles, on the other hand, seem to come from the turn of the century, when Christianity had already entered its second generation after the deaths of the Apostles, and the expectation of the Second Coming was beginning to recede from people's minds as an imminent event. The emphasis thus shifted from the charismatic type of community we glimpse in the mid-first century, to the formation of a more institutionalised structure to fit the changing circumstances faced by a growing church. These included the normalising of relations with wider society, a process which was destined to last until the late fourth century, and the clarification of doctrine and discipline, the twin safeguards against deviation and excess.

In addressing the social issues arising from the consequences of the famine of 368, Basil extended the idea of community, which had characterised the earliest groups of Christians and marked out their solidarity with the oppressed and marginalised. His identification of 'community' with society as a whole, transformed the concept of responsibility both in personal and corporate terms, and changed the way in which the Church looked at the world, and the way in which the world came to regard the Church. The impact of the one upon the other was to have far-reaching ramifications.

Early Christian ideas of community, from the New Testament to the Cappadocian Fathers, have been used at various times as models for the development of an ideological concept, enshrining basic principles and values, and providing a system of belief which reinforces people's sense of identity and belonging. Examples of this, first of all from two very different types of closed Christian community, each sharing a similar ethos of corporate responsibility and single-mindedness, would be coenobitic monasticism, on the one hand, and the Amish, a strict American Mennonite sect, on the other. At the heart of both is a total commitment to a communal-living dimension in Christianity, through a clearly defined social structure of exclusive membership, thus bearing some features characteristic of the pre-Constantinian church, and not implying that either failed to recognise an outreach function towards society. The coenobitic monasteries founded by Pachomius and Basil had a clear social thrust and included resources for the care of the sick and of travellers. A very different example, illustrating the modern church's desire for openness and inclusion, was the attempt to re-assess its role within the wider community and, at the same time, to revitalise its ministry in the decades following World War II, through the worker-priest movement. The Church was to be seen as being in the world by becoming part of the world, open that is to social inclusion and the breaking down of hitherto insuperable barriers between clergy and people. It is extremely doubtful whether in Britain this had more than a marginal effect upon society's perception of the Church as a radical, socially-conscious organisation, though much greater success was achieved by Catholic worker-priests in, say, South America, and elsewhere in areas of multi-deprivation in the Third World. The social changes, which took place in 1960s Britain and sparked off the rapid growth of the social sciences, were also the result of this process of re-evaluating the meaning of community in the modern world. At one level this became a quest for alternative types of community, which formed part of a wider protest movement against what was felt to be the rigid and authoritarian structures of society, of which the institutional church was seen to be part. In fact these movements were, and still are, as much about individualism, as about community; individuality being expressed in a communal dimension which was essentially anti-authoritarian and anti-establishment, but owing its inspiration, at least in part, to the achievements of the great social reformers of the first half of the twentieth century.

Basil and his contemporaries would probably not have understood the debate about individualism versus community which has dominated much modern social policy thinking in the last fifty years. For them, community responsibility was simply individual responsibility writ large. Basil's strictures against those who hoarded their wealth and failed to respond to urgent human need were directed at the rich as a class, but also as individuals, who would in many instances have been known personally to him. In late twentieth-century Britain, particularly in the last ten years, the debate focused on the respective responsibilities of the individual and the state to make adequate provision for health and social care. The state, and therefore each community, is increasingly seen as the safety-net for the most vulnerable in society, whilst those with greater personal resources are encouraged to invest them in their own future. At the same time, the unprecedented expansion of the charitable sector has reminded an affluent society of its duty to care for the very disparate needs of people in adversity. These are themes which our early Christian forebears would have recognised and with which they would have felt sympathy. Care in the community, then as now, concerns the rights and responsibilities of individuals towards one another and therefore to society at large.[1] Perhaps Basil and the great Christian pastors of the Patristic Age still have something to say.

NOTES

1. For an explanation of the rise of Christianity in the first four centuries AD using social-scientific concepts, the reader's attention is drawn to *The Rise of Christianity: A Sociologist Reconsiders History* by Rodney Stark (see Select Bibliography). An excellent critique of this work is to be found in the article by Todd E. Klutz, 'The Rhetoric of Science in "The Rise of Christianity": a response to Rodney Stark's Sociological Account of Christianization', *Journal of Early Christian Studies*, 16 (Summer 1998) 2 pp. 162–184, Johns Hopkins University Press. In particular, the reader should note Stark's argument about the Christian ethic of love, surviving disaster, etc. The same edition of the Journal also includes articles by other scholars assessing Stark's work, as well as Stark's own response to these.

Select Bibliography

ANCIENT SOURCES

Ante Nicene Fathers (A.N.F.), ed. by Roberts and Donaldson, Hendrickson Publishers Inc, Peabody, Mass, 1994.
Nicene and Post Nicene Fathers, First Series (N.P.N.F. 1), ed. by Philip Schaff, Hendrickson Publishers Inc, Peabody, Mass, 1995.
Nicene and Post Nicene Fathers, Second Series (N.P.N.F. 2), ed. by P. Schaff and H. Wace, Hendrickson Publishers Inc, Peabody, Mass, 1994.
Apostolic Fathers, ed. by J. B. Lightfoot, Macmillan & Co, 1891.
Ammianus Marcellinus, *The Later Roman Empire (AD 354–378)*, Penguin Classics, 1986.
Early Christian Writings – The Apostolic Fathers, trans. by Maxwell Staniforth, Penguin Classics, 1981.
Eusebius of Caesarea, *Ecclesiastical History* and *The Martyrs of Palestine*, trans. by Lawlor and Oulton, London, SPCK, 1954. See also N.P.N.F. 2, vol. 1.
Josephus, *The Jewish War*, trans. by G. A. Williamson, Penguin Classics, 1959 revised by E. Mary Smallwood, 1981.
Josephus, *The Life* and *Against Apion*, trans. by H. St. J. Thackeray, Loeb Classical Library, 1961.

MODERN WORKS

Barnes, T. D., *Constantine and Eusebius*, Cambridge, Mass, Harvard University Press, 1981.

Benko, Stephen, *Pagan Rome and the Early Christians*, London, Batsford, 1985.
Bettenson, Henry, ed., *The Early Christian Fathers*, London, Oxford University Press, 1956.
Bettenson, Henry, *The Later Christian Fathers*, Oxford, Oxford University Press, 1970.
Bettenson, Henry, *Documents of the Christian Church*, London, Oxford University Press, 1959.
Boardman, J., Griffin, J. and Murray, O., eds., *The Roman World*, Oxford History of the Classical World, Oxford, Oxford University Press, 1986.
Bowerstock, G. W., *Hellenism in Late Antiquity*, Jerome Lectures, Cambridge, Cambridge University Press, 1990.
Brown, Peter, *The World of Late Antiquity*, London, Thames & Hudson, 1971.
Brown, Peter, *The Making of Late Antiquity*, Cambridge, Mass, Harvard University Press, 1978.
Brown, Peter, 'Late Antiquity', in *A History of Private Life from Pagan Rome to Byzantium*, ed. by Paul Veyne, Cambridge, Mass, The Belknap Press, University of Harvard Press, 1987.
Brown, Peter, 'The Rise and Function of the Holy Man in Late Antiquity, 1971–1997', *Journal of Early Christian Studies*, North American Patristics Society, Fall 1998, vol. 6, no. 3, Johns Hopkins University Press, 1998.
Cambridge Medieval History, vol. 1, *The Christian Empire*, Cambridge, Cambridge University Press, 1911.
Cameron, Averil, *Christianity and the Rhetoric of Empire*, Berkeley, University of California Press, 1991.
Cameron, Averil, *The Later Roman Empire*, Fontana History of the Ancient World, London, Fontana Press, 1993.
Cameron, Averil, *The Mediterranean World in Late Antiquity, AD 395–600*, London, Routledge, 1993.
Carcopino, Jerome, *Daily Life in Ancient Rome*, London, Penguin Books, 1991.
Chadwick, Henry, *The Early Church*, Pelican History of the Church, 1, London, Penguin Books, 1967.
Cross, F. L., *The Early Christian Fathers*, London, Duckworth, 1960.
Finely, M. I., *The Ancient Economy*, Berkeley and Los Angeles,

University of California Press, 1973; 2nd edition with supplementary notes, Harmondsworth, Penguin Books, 1985.
Fowden, Garth, *Empire to Commonwealth; Consequences of monotheism in Late Antiquity*, Princeton, Princeton University Press, 1993.
Grant, Michael, *The World of Rome*, London, Weidenfeld & Nicolson, 1960.
Grant, Michael, *The Climax of Rome*, London, Weidenfeld Paperback, 1993.
Grant, Michael, *The Emperor Constantine*, London, Weidenfeld & Nicolson, 1993.
Grant, Robert, *Early Christianity and Society*, London, Collins, 1978.
Grant, Robert, *Gods and the One God*, London, SPCK, 1986.
Hazlett, Ian, ed., *Early Christianity*, London, SPCK, 1991.
Hengel, Martin, *Earliest Christianity*, trans. from the German by John Bowden, London, SCM Press, 1979.
Herrin, Judith, *The Formation of Christendom*, London, Fontana Press, 1989.
Jones, A. H. M., *The Decline of the Ancient World*, New York, Longman Inc, 1966.
Kee, Alistair, *Constantine versus Christ: The Triumph of Ideology*, London, SCM Press, 1982.
Lane Fox, Robin, *Pagans and Christians*, Harmondsworth, Viking Press, 1986.
Lietzman, Hans, *A History of the Early Church*, vols 1–4, London, Lutterworth Press, 1961.
Levy, Thomas E., ed., *Archaeology of Society in the Holy Land*, London, Leicester University Press, 1995.
MacMullen, R., *Christianizing the Roman Empire, AD 100–400*, New Haven, Yale University Press, 1984.
Meeks, Wayne, *The Moral World of the First Christians*, London, SPCK, 1987.
Pagels, Elaine, *The Gnostic Gospels*, London, Penguin Books, 1982.
Prestige, G. L., *Fathers and Heretics*, The Bampton Lectures for 1940, London, SPCK, 1958.
Ricciotti, Giuseppe, *The Age of Martyrs: Christianity from Diocletian to Constantine*, trans. by Anthony Bull, New York, Barnes & Noble, 1992.

Sordi, Marta, *The Christians and the Roman Empire*, trans. by Annabel Bedini, London, Routledge, 1988.
Stambaugh, John, and Balch, David, *The Social World of the First Christians*, London, SPCK, 1986.
Stark, Rodney, *The Rise of Christianity: A Sociologist Reconsiders History*, Princeton, Princeton University Press, 1996.
Theissen, Gerd, *The Social Setting of Pauline Christianity*, Edinburgh, T. & T. Clark, 1982.
Veyne, Paul, *Bread and Circuses*, trans. by Brian Pearce, Allen Lane, The Penguin Press, 1976.
Vogt, Joseph, *The Decline of Rome: The Metamorphosis of Ancient Civilisation*, trans. from the German by Janet Sondheimer, London, Weidenfeld & Nicolson, 1993.
Waddell, Helen, *The Desert Fathers*, London, Fontana Press, 1962.
Wallace-Hadrill, Andrew, ed., *Patronage in Ancient Society*, London, Routledge, 1989.
Williams, R., *Arius: Heresy and Tradition*, London, Darton, Longman & Todd, 1987.
Witherington, B., *Women in the Earliest Churches*, Cambridge, Cambridge University Press, 1988.

Index

Abraham 4
Achaia 27
Acts of the Apostles 16, 17, 30, 32
Agapē 65
Aegean Sea 56
Aelia Capitolina 12, 19, 55
Africa 80
Agrippa 8, 9, 19
Akkadians 2
Alexander Severus 26, 75, 81
Alexander the Great 4, 15, 23
Alexandria 4, 80, 84, 105
alms, almsgiving 51, 57, 58, 61, 64, 70, 82, 85, 95, 105, 114
Amish 117
Amorites 2
Ananias and Sapphira 44
Antioch 4, 19, 46, 75, 103
Antiochus III 5
Antiochus IV Epiphanes 5
Antipater 7
Antonines xiv, 66, 74, 78, 106
Antony 107
Apostles 60, 104, 117
Arameans 2

Archelaus 7
Arians 105, 110
Aristides 62, 89
Arius 88, 105
Arles, Council of 105
Arrian 91
asceticism 107–9
Asia Minor xiii, xiv, 30, 32, 35, 56, 60, 74, 76, 79
Assyrians 2
Athenagorus 91
Athens 89
Augustus xii, 8, 10, 19, 76
Aurelian 76

Babylonians 2
Balkans 76, 105
banking arrangements 58–9, 82, 95, 96
'Bar-Kochba', Simon 12, 30
Barnabas xi, 37, 46
Basil of Caesarea 26, 102, 114, 115, 116, 119
Bithynia 15, 86
Britain 75, 86
Byzantium 103
Byzantine Empire 40, 112

Caesarea 23, 80, 102
Caledonia 100

Index   125

Callistus 59, 95, 96–7
Canaan 2
Cappadocia 94, 114
Caracalla 76
Carpophorus 95
Carthage 94, 104
Carus 75
Cassius Dio 11
celibacy 91
Celsus 66
Chalcis 8
charity, charitable relief
   21–2, 26–8, 34, 45,
   52–3, 58, 61–2, 77, 84,
   94, 103, 106, 109, 115
Chrysopolis, Battle of 102
Claudius 8, 18
Clement of Alexandria 91
Clement of Rome 57, 60
Cleopatra 76
cliens, clientela 20, 106
Colossae 57
Commodus 58, 66, 93, 95
community, concepts of 69,
   71, 114–9
'community organisers' 21,
   37
Constantine the Great xv,
   56, 79, 84, 92, 98, 100,
   101, 102–4, 107, 108,
   110–12
Constantinople 103, 111
Constantius Chlorus 84, 86,
   100
Corinth 47, 57
Corinthians 27, 57
Cornelius, Bishop of Rome
   93
Cumanus 9
Cyprian 89, 94

Dalmatia 83
Damascus 6
Damasus, Pope 92
Decapolis 6, 23
Decius, Emperor 75, 81, 82
Diaspora xi, 15, 30, 33, 39,
   53
Didache 50–3, 60
Diocletian 34, 83–4, 85,
   86–7, 111
Dionysius, Bishop of
   Alexandria 84
Domitian 40
Donatists 104, 110

ecological factors 18
Egypt 1, 2, 30, 76, 79
Elagabals 78, 81
Eleazar 9
Ephesus 56, 90
Epictetus 91
Epiphanius of Salamis 88
Eucharist 58, 60, 61, 65, 95
euergetism 20
Euphrates 2, 4
Eusebius 11, 80, 81, 84, 94,
   103, 105, 109

Fabianus, Pope 93
Fabius, Bishop of Antioch
   93
Felix 9
Fertile Crescent 1, 2, 18
Festus 9
Flavia Neapolis 61
Flavian dynasty xiv
frumentum (grain dole) 35,
   67, 103, 105

Gabinius 6

Gaius Caligula 8
Galba 10
Galen 74, 90
Galerius 76, 84, 85, 86, 87, 102
Galilee 7, 10, 30
Gallienus 76, 82, 85, 87
Gangra, Council of 92
Gaul 75, 86
Gennesaret, Sea of 22
Gentiles 27–8, 38, 55–6
Gessius Florus 9
Gnosticism 57–8, 59, 79
Gordian 82
Goths 75
Greece/Greeks x, 5–6, 32, 56
Gregory the Great 112, 115
Gregory of Nazianzus 102, 104

Hadrian 11, 12, 55, 111
Haran 4
Hasmoneans 5–7
Hebrew Scriptures 5
Helena 107
Hellenism 4, 15
Hermas 69–70
Herod the Great 7, 18, 19
Herodeion 11
Hierocles 86
Hippolytus 95–6
Hyrcanus 7

Ignatius of Antioch 56, 58, 60
Iraq 1
Irenaeus of Lyons 92, 96
Israel 2, 15
Israelites 4
Italy 76

James the Less 17
Jerusalem xi, xii, 5, 6, 8, 9, 11, 14, 17, 18, 19, 21, 22, 23, 27, 28, 30, 31, 32, 46, 55
Jesus xiii, 16, 19, 21, 23, 28, 29, 30, 31, 42–4, 55, 58, 60, 65, 106
Jesus Movement xi, xiii, 17, 18, 21, 23–4, 29, 31, 47, 106, 107
Jews 15, 30, 31, 55, 114
John, St 31
John of Damascus 92
Josephus 9, 10, 11, 19
Joshua 22
Jotapata, seige of 9
Jovian 105
Judaea 2, 6, 7, 8, 12, 16, 17
Judaism xi, 4, 5, 14, 23, 28, 30, 31, 33, 43, 55, 57
Julian the Apostate 78, 90, 110
Julio-Claudian dynasty xiv
Jupiter 12
Justin Martyr 61
Justinian 111, 112

kerygma 29, 32

Lactantius 85, 86, 87
law enforcement 15–17
Leonidas 80
Licinius 102, 103
'love-communism' 28, 44, 46–7
'love-patriarchalism' 28, 29, 49
Lucian 62, 63
Lucius Verus 66

Maccabean Brothers 5
Macedonia 27
Machaerus 11
Magnesia 56
Manichaeism 79
Marcia 95
Marcion, heretic 61
Marcus Aurelius 66, 93, 111
martyrdom 56, 64
Masada 11
Matthew's Gospel 116
Maximian 84
Maximinus 81
Maximinus II Daia 102
Mennonites 117
Menes 2
Mesopotamia 1–2
Milan, Edict of 102
Milvian Bridge, Battle of 100
ministry, types of 60–1
Mithraism 79
Montanism 59
Mosaic Law 4, 11, 14, 17, 23, 30

Nabateans 6–7
Nablus 61
Neo-Platonists 86
Nero 10, 40, 79
New Testament 116
Nicea, Council of 105
Nicomedia 87
Novatian Schism 94
Numerian 83

Odenathus 75
Odoacer 111
Olympic Games 63
Origen 80–1, 84

Orontes 4

Pachomius 107, 118
paganism 78, 85
Palestine xi, xii, 2, 4, 5, 12, 17, 18, 23, 28, 30, 55
Palmyra 75
Parthians 7, 75
Patristic Age xiii, 119
patronage 20, 34, 106
Paul, St xi, xiii, xiv, 15, 26–7, 32, 37, 46, 47, 48, 55, 56, 60, 69, 93
Pax Romana xi, xii, 19, 77
Pella 6
Peraea 7
Peregrinus Proteus 62–3
persecution 79–83, 86–8
Persia 85
Persians 76
Peter, St xiii, 55, 93
Petra 7
Philadelphia 56
Philip the Arab 82
Philippi 57
Piscina Publica 95
Picts 100
Plato 61, 101
Platonism 57, 86
Pliny the Younger 15
Plotinus 86
Polycarp 57, 96
Pompey 6
Pontius Pilate 16, 19
Porphyry 86
poverty 47, 114, 115
Praetorian Guard 100
property and riches, 44, 47, 64, 69–70, 107
Pseudo-Clement 57

Ptolemy 4
Pythagoreans 61

Rabbinical teaching 4
Rhoda 69
Roman army 76
Rome x, 5–12, 14–7, 20, 27,
    33, 38, 56, 59, 67, 75,
    78–9, 93, 97, 112
Romulus Augustulus 111

Sabellius 97
Sadducean Priesthood 11
Samaria 2, 7
Sanhedrin 11, 16
Sassanid dynasty 75
Second Coming 117
Seleucids 4, 6
Seleucus IV 5
Septimius Severus 66, 80,
    96
Septuagint 5
Severan dynasty 66, 74, 78,
    81, 85, 106
sexual morals 90–2, 102
Shapur I, King of Kings 75
Shechem 61
Skythopolis 6
Smyrna 56, 96
Socrates 62
Sol Invictus 101
Soranus 90
Spain 75
Split 87
Stephen, St 16, 39
Sumerians 2
Syria 1, 4, 62

Talmud 22, 44

Tarsus 32
Temple xii, 5, 6, 8, 9, 11,
    14, 16, 19, 21, 22, 55,
    117
Tertullian 64, 65, 66, 89, 91
Tetrarchy 84, 86
Theodosius the Great 111
Theodoret of Cyrrhus 103
Tigris 2
Titus xii, 10, 18, 55
Tivoli 76
Torah 22
Trajan 11, 15
Tralles 56
treasure or community chest
    25, 35, 48, 58, 64, 77,
    87, 95, 106

Ubaid 2
Ulpian 26
Ur of the Chaldees 2, 4

Valentinus 110
Valerian, Emperor 75, 82,
    84
Vespasian 9, 10

'wandering (itinerant)
    charismatics' 21, 36–7,
    45, 46, 60
women, role of 76, 106–7

York 100

Zealots xii, 44
Zeus Olympios 5
Zenobia 75
Zephyrinus 96
Zoroastrianism 57